In the Words of Nelson Mandela

In the Words of
Nelson Mandela

Compiled and edited by
Jennifer Crwys-Williams

WALKER & CO.
NEW YORK

Published by Walker Publishing Company, Inc., New York

All papers used by Walker & Company are natural, recyclable products made from wood grown in well-managed forests. The manufacturing processes conform to the environmental regulations of the country of origin.

LIBRARY OF CONGRESS CATALOGING-IN-PUBLICATION DATA HAS BEEN APPLIED FOR.

ISBN: 978-0-8027-7930-4

Visit Walker & Company's Web site at www.walkerbooks.com

First published in Great Britain in 2010 by Profile Books Ltd. (UK)
First published in the United States by Walker & Company in 2011

1 3 5 7 9 10 8 6 4 2

Printed in the U.S.A. by Quad/Graphics, Fairfield, Pennsylvania

This book is dedicated to the children of South Africa in the hope that as they grow they may find inspiration from the thoughts of Nelson Rolihlahla Mandela – and that, in his words on receiving the Nobel Peace Prize, they and other children the world over, may 'play in the open veld, no longer tortured by the pangs of hunger or ravaged by disease or threatened with the scourge of ignorance, molestation and abuse ... children are the greatest of our treasures.' In particular, I hope this little book inspires the children in my own family, living in both the old and the new worlds: Amber, Cassandra, Sebastian, Phoebe and Blaise.

Acknowledgements

My special thanks to the journalists who, over the years, have interviewed Nelson Mandela and who have provided me with much of the material used in this book. It is no exaggeration to say that without their help this book would not have been possible.

I received substantial amounts of help for the first edition of this book from Susan Segar, then political correspondent of *The Natal Witness*.

Thanks too to Carole Blake of Blake Friedmann & Associates, who has been generous with her support and interest.

Introduction

Nelson Mandela is the world's role model. He has been described as 'the world's last great super-hero', 'an icon of forgiveness, compassion, magnanimity and reconciliation for the entire globe', 'a myth', 'an icon of righteousness', and, by Bill Clinton when celebrating his eighty-fifth birthday in July 2003, 'You have taught us the freedom of forgiveness, the futility of coercive power ... and the joy of service.' His wife, Graça Machel, has said pointedly that 'he is a symbol but not a saint'.

However he is described, he has become a towering symbol of reconciliation and sacrifice. Above all, he is perceived as a man who did his duty.

With the reach and might of twenty-first-century communications, the myth of the man sometimes conceals the very real human being who exists beneath the hyperbole. How better, then, to let Nelson Mandela speak for himself in his own unembellished words?

Perhaps his thoughts, reproduced on these pages, and honed over many years of tribulation, will inspire people, young and old, monied and impoverished, the world over.

In particular, I hope it will inspire people who have had few role models in their lives, and who have suffered their own apartheids in their own countries.

Jennifer Crwys-Williams

*'I will continue fighting for freedom
until the end of my days.'*

on abortion

Women have the right to decide what they want to do with their bodies.

on his achievements

Don't tempt me to beat my chest and to say this is what I have done!

In spite of interviewers the world over hoping for intimate revelations, Nelson Mandela dislikes speaking about himself and invariably refers to the 'collective' – meaning, of course, the African National Congress

I must not be isolated from the collective who are responsible for the success. *my failure*

When I make a mistake, I normally say: 'It's these young chaps,' and when they do something good, I say: 'This is the man.'

To illustrate his point, Madiba beat his chest – this was in an internationally televised interview, December 1997: Mandela Meets the Media

on Africa

For centuries, an ancient continent has bled from many gaping sword wounds.

No doubt Africa's renaissance is at hand – and our challenge is to steer the continent through the tide of history.

The people of the continent are eager and willing to be among the very best in all areas of endeavour.

The peoples of resurgent Africa are perfectly capable of deciding upon their own future form of government and discovering and themselves dealing with any dangers which might arise.

We need to exert ourselves that much more, and break out of the vicious cycle of dependence imposed on us by the financially powerful; those in command of immense market power and those who dare to fashion the world in their own image.

Africa, more than any other continent, has had to contend with the consequences of conquest in a denial of its own role in history, including the denial that its people had the capacity to bring about change and progress.

It would be a cruel irony of history if Africa's actions to regenerate the continent were to unleash a new scramble for Africa which, like that of the nineteenth century, plundered the continent's wealth and left it once more the poorer.

Conflict threatens not only the gains we have made but also our collective future.

The African rebirth is now more than an idea – its seeds are being sown in the regional communities we are busy building and in the continent as a whole.

Can we continue to tolerate our ancestors being shown as people locked in time?

Africa yearns and deserves to redeem her glory, to reassert her centuries-old contribution to economics, politics, culture and the arts; and once more to be a pioneer in the many fields of human endeavour.

One destabilising conflict anywhere on the continent is one too many.

For as long as the majority of people anywhere on the continent feel oppressed, are not allowed democratic participation in decision-making processes, and cannot elect their own leaders in free and fair elections, there will always be tension and conflict.

A continent which, while it led in the very evolution of human life and was a leading centre of learning, technology and the arts in ancient times, has experienced various traumatic epochs, each one of which has pushed her peoples deeper into poverty and backwardness.

We cannot abuse the concept of national sovereignty to deny the rest of the continent the right and duty to intervene when, behind those sovereign boundaries, people are being slaughtered to protect tyranny. *R2P*

He said this in June 1998 in his address to the Organisation of African Unity

We should treat the question of peace and stability on our continent as a common challenge.

Africa has long traversed past a mindset that seeks to heap all blame on the past and on others.

---

on being an African

Teach the children that Africans are not one iota inferior to Europeans.

From his seminal 'No Easy Walk to Freedom' speech, 21 August 1953

The lack of human dignity experienced by Africans is the direct result of the policy of white supremacy.

Spoken from the dock at the Rivonia Treason Trial, 20 April 1964, which sent him to prison for 27 long years

All of us, descendants of Africa, know only too well that racism demeans the victims and dehumanizes its perpetrators.

We are rising from the ashes of war.

He said this while presenting the Africa Peace Award to the war-torn country of Mozambique in November 1997. Madiba's wife, Graça Machel, is the widow of the former president of that country and he feels a great bond with it

on the African National Congress

As no man is an island, so too are we not men of stone who are unmoved by the noble passions of love, friendship and human compassion.

He was referring to the formation of the ANC Youth League on Easter Sunday, 1944. Mandela and his lifelong friends Oliver Tambo and Walter Sisulu, were prominent among its founding fathers – the young Turks of their day. This

*quotation was from a speech made in Uppsala
Cathedral, Sweden, in March 1990*

We must move from the position of a resistance
movement to one of builders.

For us the struggle against racism has assumed
the proportions of a crusade.

The African National Congress is the greatest
achievement of the twentieth century.

*From an interview in 1997, the year he
relinquished his presidency of the party*

I have always been a member of the African
National Congress and I will remain a member of
the African National Congress until I die.

---

on the African Renaissance

As we dream and work for the regeneration of our
continent, we remain conscious that the African
Renaissance can only succeed as part of the development of a new and equitable world order in
which all the formerly colonised and marginalised
take their rightful place, makers of history rather
than the possessions of others.

As we stand on the threshold of a new African
era characterised by democracy, sustainable economic development and a re-awakening of our

rich cultural values and heritage, African unity remains our watchword and the Organisation of African Unity our guide.

---

on Afrikaners

As those who drew benefits from a previous programme of affirmative action, they should realise better than anyone else how such a programme can contribute towards making the community more productive.

I have often noticed Afrikaans people remark that the new South Africa gives them a feeling of freedom now that they have entered a wider world of relationships with fellow South Africans.

Maybe it was out of fear that they themselves would one day become the oppressed once again.

On possible reasons for the Afrikaners oppressing fellow South Africans during apartheid, and spoken in the tense run-up to South Africa's first democratic election in 1994

When you speak Afrikaans, you go straight to their hearts.

When an Afrikaner changes, he changes) completely.

Many Afrikaners, who once acted with great cruelty and insensitivity towards the majority in our country, to an extent you have to go to jail to understand, have changed completely and become loyal South Africans in whom one can trust.

---

on age

What nature has decreed should not generate undue insecurity.

I am nearing my end. I want to be able to sleep until eternity with a broad smile on my face, knowing that the youth, opinion-makers and everybody is stretched across the divide, trying to unite the nation.

From a speech to students at the University of Potchefstroom, February 1996. He was then 77. Nelson Mandela was born in the tiny Transkei village of Mvezo on 18 July 1918

I will be 81 when I finally retire, and I never thought a man in his 70s should take over an organisation like the ANC.

The autumn of our lives presages the African spring.

He said this in Ouagadougou, Burkina Faso, addressing the Organisation of African Unity.

*He celebrated his 80th birthday at home in
Johannesburg with his family on 18 July 1998*

One of the advantages of old age is that people
respect you because of your grey hair and say
all manner of nice things about you that are not
based on who you really are.

I only keep myself busy so that I can prove that
although I'm a has-been, I've still got some work
to do.

*Said in 2002, when he was 84 and as busy
as ever*

To be an old man is very nice because, as a young
man, I didn't get the support I am getting now.

*He recounted the $10 million given to him
by TV talk-show host Oprah Winfrey, and a
number of banks whom he phoned at intervals
of 15 minutes, raising enough money to send
20 young people to university. The occasion was
the launch in Johannesburg, July 2003, of the
Mindset Network educational project. Nelson
Mandela joked that the first thing he would do
when he reached the 'next world' would be to
ferret out the billionaires. 'I am going to say to
them "raise money" because I know the poor
are everywhere and these children need to go to
school.'*

on aids

Aids is clearly a disaster, effectively wiping out the development gains of the past decades and sabotaging the future.

Nelson Mandela was closing the 13th International Aids conference in Durban, July 2000, and drew a standing ovation

The challenge is to move from rhetoric to action, and action at an unprecedented intensity and scale.

There is no shame to disclose a terminal disease from which you are suffering.

He said this in 2002, after making a deliberate gesture by publicly embracing HIV-infected Aids activist Zackie Achmat; he also disclosed that three members of his own family had died of Aids. He was criticised by a prominent gay HIV-positive South African judge, Edwin Cameron, for failing to give a message on Aids when he was president. 'In 199 ways, he was our country's saviour. In the 200th way, he was not.'

Those who are infected with this terrible disease do not want stigma, they want love.

On the fifth anniversary of the death of Britain's Princess Diana (31 August 2002), he paid special tribute to her work in smashing the

*superstitions surrounding the disease. He noted
that she had gone to hospitals with Aids patients,
sitting on their beds and shaking hands. 'We have
to continue to break that stigma,' he noted at the
time*

We must not continue to be debating, to be
arguing, when people are dying. *going extinct*
species

This is a global injustice. It is a travesty of human
rights on a global scale.

*Nelson Mandela in Paris, July 2003. He was
speaking about the cost of life-saving medicine
for poor Aids sufferers*

I was just a number. Millions of people today
infected with Aids are classified as just a number.
They too are serving a prison sentence for life.

*Nelson Mandela launched his 46664 Give One
Minute of Your Life to Aids campaign in October
2003. The culmination of the campaign was the
46664 concert at Green Point Stadium, Cape
Town, on 29 November 2003*

A tragedy of unprecedented proportions is unfold-
ing in Africa.

*This statement was a precursor to the 46664
concert for Aids. People worldwide were urged
to phone 082 1 46664 to listen to music –
and raise money for the fight against the dread
disease*

Aids today in Africa is claiming more lives than the sum total of all wars, famines and floods and the ravages of such deadly diseases as malaria.

I had no idea when I started this campaign that it would affect a member of my family ... I have called you here today to announce that my son has died of Aids.

A visibly saddened Nelson Mandela said this on 6 January 2004 at his Houghton home, telling the world about the death of his 54 year-old son, Makgatho Mandela. Makgatho's second wife, Joyce Zondi, also died in 2004, of pneumonia

The only way to make it appear like a normal illness like TB and cancer is to come out and say somebody died because of HIV/Aids, and people will stop regarding it as an extraordinary illness reserved for people who go to hell instead of heaven.

Madiba, explaining why he had made public the cause of his son's death

I would love to enjoy the peace and quiet of retirement but I know that, like many of you, I cannot rest while our beloved continent is ravaged by a deadly epidemic.

Nelson Mandela at his second 46664 concert for Aids relief. It was held in Cape Town in March 2005

For every woman infected by HIV, we destroy a generation.

---

on alliances

No **true alliance** can be built on the shifting sands of evasions, illusions, and opportunism.

---

on anger

Anger is a temporary feeling – you soon forget it, particularly if you are involved in positive activities and attitudes.

---

on apartheid

Apartheid is the rule of the gun and the hangman.

The universal struggle against apartheid was not an act of charity arising out of pity for our people, but an affirmation of our common humanity.

Out of the experience of an extraordinary human disaster that lasted too long, must be born a society of which all humanity will be proud.

At his inauguration as President of South Africa, 10 May 1994

It would have been immoral to keep quiet while a racist tyranny sought to reduce an entire people into a status worse than that of beasts of the forest.

The millions of graves strewn across Europe which are the result of the tyranny of Nazism, the decimation of the native peoples of the Americas and Australia, the destructive trail of the apartheid regime against humanity – all these are like a haunting question that floats in the wind: why did we allow these to happen?

Apartheid continues to live with us in the leaking roofs and corrugated walls of shacks; in the bulging stomachs of hungry children; in the darkness of homes without electricity; and in the heavy pails of dirty water that rural women carry for long distances to cook and to quench their thirst.

He said this in November 1997, one month before stepping down as president of the ANC

At each turn of history, apartheid was bound to spawn resistance; it was destined to bring to life the forces that would guarantee its death. P13

With the exception of the atrocities against the Jews during World War II, there is no evil that has been as condemned by the entire world as apartheid.

*He was speaking in December 1998, his last full
year as President of South Africa*

The struggle against apartheid can be typified as
the pitting of remembering against forgetting.

---

on appearances

Appearances constitute reality.

---

on a Bill of Rights

A Bill of Rights is an important statement about
the nature of power relations in any society.

The ANC has had a Bill of Rights since 1923

A Bill of Rights cannot be associated with the
political or economic subordination of either the
majority or the minority.

A Bill of Rights is a living thing.

---

on being a black man in a white man's court (1962)

I hate race discrimination most intensely and in
all its manifestations. Even though I now happen
to be tried by one whose opinion I hold in high
esteem, I detest most violently the set-up that

surrounds me here. It makes me feel that I am a black man in a white man's court.

Nelson Mandela appeared in the Old Synagogue in Pretoria from 15 October–7 November 1962 following his arrest in August after being on the run for 17 months. Hand-written first drafts of many of his political speeches written before he went to prison exist – but not the most famous one of all, spoken at the Rivonia Trial, because his 'I am prepared to die' speech was a collaborative effort

When my sentence has been completed I will still be moved, as men are always moved, by their consciences; I will still be moved by my dislike of the race discrimination against my people when I come out from serving my sentence, to take up again, as best I can, the struggle for the removal of those injustices until they are finally abolished once and for all.

Spoken in court, on 7 November 1962, at the end of his 'Synagogue' trial when he was convicted and sentenced to three years' imprisonment on charges of incitement and two years' imprisonment for leaving South Africa without valid travel documents

on black consciousness

In various forms and under various labels, this attitude of mind and way of life have coursed through the veins of all the motive forces of struggle.

Black consciousness has fired the determination of leaders and the masses alike.

The driving thrust of black consciousness was to forge pride and unity amongst all the oppressed, to foil the strategy of divide-and-rule, to engender pride among the mass of our people and confidence in their ability to throw off their oppression.

Above all, the liberation movement asserted that the people would most readily develop consciousness of their proud being, of their equality with everyone else, of their capacity to make history.

The value that black consciousness placed on culture reverberated across our land; in our prisons; and amongst the communities in exile – and our people, who were once enjoined to look to Europe and America for creative sustenance, turned their eyes to Africa.

*Nelson Mandela was commemorating the death
of black consciousness leader Steve Biko*

on black South Africans

The blacks think this transformation was brought about by military victory, and they have defeated the whites. They think the whites are lying on the floor and begging for mercy.

From an interview during his July 1996 state visit to Britain

on his 80th birthday

Life will go on as normal.

But Nelson Mandela was being disingenuous. He had made plans to marry the former wife of the late president of Mozambique, Graça Machel. Only a handful of people knew and they kept the secret until the marriage was announced on Mandela's birthday

I feel very well. I feel on top of the world.

Madiba was speaking to journalists from the Sowetan just before his birthday. He told them he had been late for his meeting because he had been exercising: 'Of course, I am not as vigorous as some of you young men, but I do my exercises every morning.'

If you live until 80 you have the respect of everybody, including those who used to despise you.

*Nelson Mandela celebrated his 80th birthday
at his home in Houghton, Johannesburg,
South Africa, by quietly marrying Graça
Machel, the former wife of the late President of
Mozambique, Samora Machel. Their marriage
delighted the world*

If I could be given another 80 years.

*This was said in response to a journalist's
question: What would you like for your
birthday?*

I have been quite overwhelmed by the expressions of good wishes. There is so much to be thankful for.

---

on his 90th birthday

After nearly 90 years of life, it is time for new hands to lift the burdens. It is in your hands now.

*Nelson Mandela had just made his slow way to
the podium for the 46664 concert in London's
Hyde Park in June 2008 in celebration of his
90th birthday on 18 July. Organised by actor
Will Smith, the stars included Johnny Clegg,
the Soweto Gospel Choir and Congolese singer
Papa Wemba. A slugfest of stars, including
Bill Clinton and Oprah Winfrey, attended a*

*separate dinner in his honour. Five years earlier,
at Mandela's 85th birthday celebration, Bill
Clinton attended his party and paying tribute
to his friend, he said: 'You have taught us the
freedom of forgiveness, the futility of coercive
power... and the joy of service.'*

Your voices carried across the water to inspire us
in our prison cells far away. Tonight, we can stand
before you free.

In front of cheering fans at the 46664 concert

I would be nothing without the ANC. The struggle
has been my life and the ANC led that struggle.

*Nelson Mandela's opening words at the ANC
rally at Loftus Versfeld Stadium, Pretoria, in
celebration of his 90th birthday. He went on to
say: 'I thank the ANC for having given meaning
to my 90 years on this planet, in this country we
all love so dearly.'*

As you know, I am not a speaker at all, and I'm
not going to make any exception on this occasion,
except to say thank you all for what you have done
for me. Thank you.

*Speaking from his family home in Qunu on
his birthday. There was a feast of traditional
dishes, together with crayfish, tiger prawn
tails, calamari and wines. Thousands of local
wellwishers, who affectionately call him 'Tata
Mkhulu', gathered outside the homestead so*

loved by him. Struggle heroes Ahmed Kathrada
and George Bizos were with him, as were
many others especially invited to celebrate his
birthday. The event was made even more special
by his grandson, the newly installed Chief
Mandla Mandela, who drove three cattle from
the rural outpost of Mvezo, the birthplace of
Nelson Mandela in the Eastern Cape, to Qunu,
some 25 km away. The cattle were a tribute
to his grandfather. Joined by five of his senior
councillors, the journey took eight hours. The
Chief wore a royal Xhosa blanket and carried a
knobkerrie. As he approached his grandfather's
house, he and his men, with the cattle in front,
passed between crowds of ululating villagers.
'We knew we had to make this journey,' he
said. He is formally known as Nkosi Zwelivelile
Mandela

---

on Bosnia

They [the leaders] thought through their blood
and not through their brains.

---

on boxing

I did not enjoy the violence of boxing as much as
the science of it.

In the ring, rank, age, colour and wealth are irrelevant.

Nelson Mandela was a heavyweight boxer himself, training every evening at Jerry Moloi's boxing gymnasium, Soweto

on boycotts

By and large, boycotts are recognised and accepted by the people as an effective and powerful weapon of political struggle.

on the British

I regard the British parliament as the most democratic institution in the world, and the independence and impartiality of its judiciary never fail to arouse my admiration.   Not Canadian

on Cairo

Africa's greatest city.

on Cape Town

It was here, three centuries ago, that sailors from Europe triggered off the chain of the dispossession whose consequences we are still grappling with today.

In Cape Town resides part of the souls of many nations and cultures, priceless threads in the rich diversity of our African nation.

The city hosted me and my colleagues for over 26 years.

Robben Island lies off the coast of Cape Town and can be clearly seen from Table Mountain. Cape Town, of course, was also the city which welcomed him on his first day of freedom

---

on the Caribbean

[The Caribbean] has, in song and verse, in political philosophy and action, long been a source for the articulation of both the lamentations and aspirations of black people everywhere.

When Africans were wrenched from their continent, they carried Africa with them and made the Caribbean a part of Africa.

---

on change

Belief in the possibility of change and renewal is perhaps one of the defining characteristics of politics and of religions.

on charity

Cash handouts might sustain you for a few months, at the end of which your problems remain.

on his childhood

When I was a boy brought up in my village in the Transkei, I listened to the elders of the tribe telling stories about the good old days, before the arrival of the white man.

In his autobiography, Long Walk to Freedom, *Mandela writes touchingly about his childhood. His collaborator on the book was* Time *contributor Richard Stengel; it took 18 months to write, starting with a manuscript Mandela had begun secretly in his prison cell. They began work daily at 6.45 am – Mandela is an early riser to this day*

I hoped and vowed then that, among the treasures that life might offer me, would be the opportunity to serve my people and make my own humble contribution to the freedom struggle.

on children

Children are the most vulnerable citizens in any society and the greatest of our treasures.

Nobel Peace Prize ceremony, Oslo, Norway
1993

The children must, at last, play in the open veld, no longer tortured by the pangs of hunger or ravaged by disease or threatened with the scourge of ignorance, molestation and abuse, and no longer required to engage in deeds whose gravity exceeds the demands of their tender years.

The children who sleep in the streets, reduced to begging to make a living, are testimony to an unfinished job.

There can be no keener revelation of a society's soul than the way in which it treats its children.

Taken from his summary of the first year of the
Nelson Mandela Children's Fund, 1996 (on
the Worldwide Web at http://www.web.co.za/
mandela/children)

The true character of a society is revealed in how it treats its children.

When you see the children, the way they are dressed, completely emaciated, you are really moved.

He was speaking about children in general, and
about the children who live around the Transkei
villages he calls home, in particular

---

on circumcision

The pain went into the marrow of my bones.

I was not as forthright and strong as the other boys that preceded me.

The fact that courage is expected of you in the face of the unbearable gives you strength for the rest of your life.

---

on clothes

My father gave me his riding breeches and he cut them, and they had twine which I used as a belt, and that is how I went to school for the first time. I had a pair of shorts, sandals but no socks, a sleeveless shirt and no underwear, which is very humiliating.

Talking to the then editor of French Vogue,
December 1993, and referring to the early
days of his imprisonment – a far cry from the
'Madiba style' shirts he has made famous. They
are generally made of silk and lined with silk –

and the pattern is perfectly aligned, making them
costly in terms of fabric to make

There isn't a single article I wear that I have
bought – people just generously give me clothes.

1994, after seven months as president

Every time I put on a bow tie I am so uncomfort-
able I can hardly talk.

Everybody just looks at my face – not at my clothes.

I use TS to promote adult public ed now!

on colonialism

The resistance of the black man to white colonial
intrusion was crushed by the gun.

Taken from Mandela's letter, smuggled out of
Robben Island after the 1976 Soweto uprising,
and published internationally by the ANC in
1980

The nineteenth-century colonisation of the
African continent was in many respects the culmination of the Renaissance-initiated expansion
of European dominion over the planet.

on communication

One of our strongest weapons is dialogue.

on communism

For many decades communists were the only political group in South Africa who were prepared to treat Africans as human beings and their equals; who were prepared to eat with us; talk with us, live with us and work with us.

Spoken from the dock at the Rivonia Treason Trial, 20 April 1964

There is so much hypocrisy behind some of this red-baiting that it sickens me, and I feel like saying to the culprits: 'How dare you say to me, a man of 75, that I must denounce my friends, and for whom?'

on compromise

That is the nature of compromising: you can compromise on fundamental issues.

At one of his first interviews after his release from 27 years' imprisonment, 15 February 1990. He was released on 11 February 1990

If you are not prepared to compromise, then you must not enter into, or think about, the process of negotiation at all.

Compromise must not undermine your own position.

Insignificant things, peripheral issues, don't need any compromise.

on conciliation

No organisation whose interests are identical with those of the toiling masses will advocate conciliation to win its demands.

on conflict

One effect of sustained conflict is to narrow our vision of what is possible.

From the 2000 Independent News & Media lecture at Trinity College, Dublin

All enduring conflicts, even if they start with right on one or other side, reach a point at which neither side is wholly right or wrong.

on the Congressional Gold Medal, USA

The award with which you honour me is an expression of the common humanity that binds us, one person to another, nation to nation, and people of the north to people of the south.

He received the medal at the Rotunda on Capitol Hill, Washington, on 23 September 1998, his last visit to the USA as President of South Africa

I receive it with pride, as a symbol of the partnership for peace, prosperity and equity as we enter the new millennium.

The medal has also been received by Mother Teresa, Winston Churchill, Thomas Edison, Walt Disney and Joe Louis among roughly 100 others

---

on the South African constitution

We give life to our nation's prayer for freedom regained and a continent reborn.

On signing the new South African constitution into law at Sharpeville, 10 December 1996

Let us now, drawing strength from the unity which we have forged, together grasp the opportunities and realise the vision enshrined in this constitution.

Respect for human life, liberty and well-being must be enshrined as rights beyond the power of any force to diminish.

on criticism

If the criticism is valid, it must be made.

on culture

Like truth, culture and creativity are enduring.

on his culture

In my culture we don't discuss personal questions with young people.

Our families are far larger than those of whites and it is always a pleasure to be fully accepted throughout a village, district, or even several districts, accompanied by your clan, and be a beloved household member, where you can call at any time, completely relaxed, sleep at ease and freely take part in the discussion of all problems, where you can even be given livestock and land to build, free of charge.

From an undated letter to his cousin Sisi, written from Robben Island

---

on the dead

In eulogies to the departed, the works of the living sometimes bear little relation to reality.

The names of only very few people are remembered beyond their lives.

---

on his death

It would be very egotistical of me to say how I would like to be remembered. I'd leave that entirely to South Africans. I would just like a simple stone on which is written, 'Mandela'.

Taken from a moving article for The New York Times *magazine by Anthony Lewis, 23 March 1997*

There will be life after Mandela.

On my last day I want to know that those who remain behind will say: 'The man who lies here has done his duty for his country and his people.'

He said this in 1999, in Qunu, where he was warmly welcomed shortly after his retirement

planet & our common
humanity

on the death sentence

The death sentence is a reflection of the animal instinct still in human beings.

wish there was more animal instinct!

on democracy

What is important is not only to attain victory for democracy, it is to retain democracy.

Democracy and human rights are inseparable.

A democratic political order must be based on the majority principle, especially in a country where the vast majority have been systematically denied their rights.

Let us never be unmindful of the terrible past from which we come – that memory not as a means to keep us shackled to the past in a negative manner, but rather as a joyous reminder of how far we have come and how much we have achieved.

He was speaking to a joint sitting of parliament, held to mark 10 years of democracy in South Africa

A guiding principle in our search for and establishment of a non-racial, inclusive democracy in our country has been that there are good men and women to be found in all groups and from all sectors of society; and that in an open and free society those South Africans will come together to jointly and cooperatively realise the common good.

To a joint sitting of parliament on 10 May 2004

Let us refrain from chauvinistic breast-beating; but let us also not underrate what we have achieved in establishing a stable and progressive democracy where we take freedoms seriously; in building national unity in spite of decades and centuries of apartheid and colonial rule; in creating a culture in which we increasingly respect the dignity of all.

on demonstrations

Mass action is a peaceful form of channelling the anger of the people.

on detention without trial

The detention without trial of political opponents is contrary to the basic principles of a democratic polity.

on determination

As long as you have an iron will you can turn misfortune into advantage.

From a letter to his daughter, Zindzi Mandela, September 1990

on what he would die for

I have fought against white domination, and I have fought against black domination. I have cherished the ideal of a democratic and free society in which all persons live together in harmony and with equal opportunities. It is an ideal which I hope to live for and to achieve. But if needs be, it is an ideal for which I am prepared to die.

Delivered from the dock at the Rivonia Treason Trial, April 1964

on discipline

Discipline is the most powerful weapon to get liberation.

An organisation can only carry out its mandate if there is discipline, and where there is no discipline there can be no real progress.

on domesticity

I make my own bed every day. I don't allow the ladies who look after me to do it. I can cook a decent meal . . . I can polish a floor.

on education

Parents have the right to choose the kind of education that shall be given to their children.

Make every home, every shack or rickety structure a centre of learning.

on election day (27 April 1994)

It was as though we were a nation reborn.

Nelson Mandela was 75 when he cast his first vote at Ohlange High School, Inanda, KwaZulu-Natal

We can loudly proclaim from the rooftops – Free at last! Free at last!

After Martin Luther King, Jnr (the closing words from his 'I Have a Dream' speech, Washington 28 August 1963). Nelson Mandela spoke the words on the first day of the first democratic South African elections, 27 April 1994

I stand before you humbled by your courage with a heart full of love for all of you.

---

on emigration

To this day we continue to lose some of the best among ourselves because the lights in the developed world shine brighter.

---

on enemies

If a man fights back he is likely to get more respect than he would if he capitulated.

At his Bishopscourt, Cape Town, press conference on 15 February 1990, his first after his release from 27 years' imprisonment

I wanted South Africa to see that I loved even my enemies while I hated the system that turned us against one another.

Mandela's presidency was notable for the efforts he made towards reconciliation – including taking tea in the all-white Boer enclave of Oranje with the widow of the architect of apartheid, Dr Hendrik Verwoerd, and meeting Dr Percy Yutar, prosecuting attorney at the Rivonia Treason Trial

on his family

I have had to separate myself from my dear wife
and children, from my mother and sisters, to live
as an outlaw in my own land.

I am convinced that your pain and suffering was
far greater than my own.

*Said during his first speech as a free man, at a
rally in Cape Town, 11 February 1990*

I did not in the beginning choose to place my
people above my family, but in attempting to serve
my people, I found I was prevented from fulfilling
my obligations as a son, a brother, a father and a
husband.

*He has said this frequently, and might have
added 'and as a grandfather'. In 1997 he had 21
grandchildren*

Our political activities have just destroyed our
family.

*Spoken after two and a half years as president
of South Africa and referring to his retirement,
which he expected to be spent largely as a global
statesman*

To see your family, your children being persecuted
when you are absolutely helpless in jail, that is

one of the most bitter experiences, most painful experiences, I have had.

Playing with [my] grandchildren makes me forget about the troubles of the world.

on fear

Our deepest fear is not that we are inadequate. Our deepest fear is that we are powerful beyond measure. As we are liberated from our own fear, our presence automatically liberates others.

on his favourite things

My favourite animal is the <u>impala</u> because it is alert, curious, rapid and able to get out of difficult conditions easily – and with grace.

Taken from French Vogue *December 1993/ January 1994. It was a historic issue – edited by Nelson Mandela himself – and now a collector's item*

Koeksisters are my favourite: in 1941 I was paid £2 a month and I reserved 10/- each weekend for koeksisters.

Koeksisters are a sticky Afrikaans sweet: plaited dough, deep fried and dunked in cold syrup. He was talking to satirist Pieter-Dirk Uys

My favourite pastime: reading.

on the football World Cup, 2010

Our time has come.

Nelson Mandela had travelled with other South African leaders to Zurich, Switzerland in May 2004, to make final representations to Fifa in anticipation of South Africa's successful bid to win the rights to the Football World Cup in 2010. Mandela was there with two South African Nobel Peace Prize laureates: FW de Klerk and Archbishop Desmond Tutu. Everyone united as South Africa's 29-minute presentation was shown

My friends, it is 28 years since Fifa took its step against racial inequality and helped inspire the final struggle against apartheid.

Nelson Mandela, of course, was South Africa's trump card

I felt like a young man of 15!

Nelson Mandela after Fifa president Sepp Blatter revealed that South Africa had won the 2010 World Cup: 'Fifa World Cup 2010: South Africa.' Desmond Tutu told a reporter: 'I want to go outside and dance, man!'

The beauty of this victory is that we were dealing with highly capable competitors who made it difficult for us to forecast what the result would be.

*Madiba turned to the dismayed Moroccan
delegation after it had lost out on the 2010
World Cup to comfort them*

on freedom

There is no easy walk to freedom.

*He was 35 when he made that statement in his
famous 'No Easy Walk to Freedom' speech. The
words were originally spoken by India's first
prime minister after independence, Jawaharlal
Nehru*

Too many have suffered for the love of freedom.

*Still imprisoned, this was from his first speech in
almost 25 years. It was read in Johannesburg to
wildly cheering crowds by his youngest daughter,
Zindzi, on 10 February 1985*

Only free men can negotiate.

*He spoke about this frequently: 'Only free men
can negotiate; prisoners cannot enter into
contracts.'*

No power on earth can stop an oppressed people
determined to win their freedom.

*From 'The Struggle is My Life' press statement,
26 June 1961*

There is no such thing as part freedom.

Only through hardship, sacrifice and militant action can freedom be won.

No South African should rest and wallow in the joy of freedom.

To men, freedom in their own land is the pinnacle of their ambitions, from which nothing can turn men of conviction aside.

We do not want freedom without bread, nor do we want bread without freedom.

To overthrow oppression is the highest aspiration of every free man.

From Mandela's 'Black Man in a White Court'
statement at his trial held in the Old Synagogue,
Pretoria, from 15 October to 7 November 1962

A man who takes away another man's freedom is a prisoner of hatred.

After 27 years' imprisonment, Nelson Mandela
walked to freedom through the gates of Victor
Verster Prison, Paarl, at 4.16 pm on 11
February 1990. He was 71

Freedom cannot be achieved unless women have been emancipated from all forms of oppression.

To be free is not merely to cast off one's chains, but to live in a way that respects and enhances the lives of others.

Our freedom is incomplete without the freedom of the Palestinians; without the resolution of conflicts in East Timor, the Sudan and other parts of the world.

The choice is not between freedom and justice on the one hand, and their opposite, on the other.

For as long as legitimate bodies of opinion feel stifled, vile minds will take advantage of justifiable grievances to destroy, to kill and to maim.

---

on the Freedom Charter (1955)

It has received international acclaim as an outstanding human rights document.

The Charter is more than a mere list of demands for democratic reforms.

---

on friendship

Friendship and support from friends is something which is a source of tremendous inspiration always and to everyone.

Those who are ready to join hands can overcome the greatest challenges.

on the future

The fall of our century will carry away the foliage of bitterness which has accumulated in our hearts, and to which colonialism, neo-colonialism and white minority domination gave birth.

You are responsible for your own future, and with hard work you can accomplish anything and make your dreams come true.

Nelson Mandela was referring to South African Idols winner Karin Kortje, whose rise from a Grabouw apple picker to the nation's songster was embraced by everyone. He was speaking in December 2005

on goals

The ways in which we will achieve our goals are bound by context, changing with circumstances even while remaining steadfast in our commitment to our vision.

Chris Hani Award at 10th National Congress of SACP, Johannesburg, 1 July 1998

on government

When a government seeks to suppress a peaceful demonstration of an unarmed people by mobilising the entire reserves of the state, military and police, it concedes powerful mass support for such a demonstration.

Said in 1961, when he was living in hiding, and was referred to as the Black Pimpernel in the nation's press. A small monument has now been erected close to the spot where he was finally arrested on the night of 5 July 1962 outside the small KwaZulu-Natal town of Howick

There is always a danger that when there is no opposition, the governing party can become too arrogant – too confident of itself.

There is nothing which makes people more appreciative of a government than that it should be able to deliver services.

on government corruption

India

Corruption in government – that is a plague that must be erased from every regime in every place in the world.

on Harlem, New York

Harlem symbolizes the strength and beauty in resistance and you have taught us that out of resistance to injustice comes renaissance, renewal and rebirth.

on hate

No one is born hating another person because of the colour of his skin, or his background, or his religion.

on health

The wounds that cannot be seen are more painful than those that can be treated by a doctor.

on heroes

No single individual can assume the role of hero or Messiah.

There are men and women chosen to bring happiness into the hearts of people – those are the real heroes.

on his heroes

Muhammed Ali was an inspiration to me even in prison because I thought of his courage and commitment. He used mind and body in unison and achieved success.

I would never miss a movie with Sophia Loren in it.

Kobie Coetsee – I have immense respect for that man because when no member of the National Party wanted to hear about the ANC, he was working systematically with me. He is one of my heroes.

Kobie Coetsee was Minister of Justice under P W Botha prior to Nelson Mandela's release on 11 February 1990

My heroes are men and women, black and white, who are worried about socio-economic questions: people like Mother Theresa and many others – these are my heroes.

He said this in a television interview with talk-show host Tim Modise on Carte Blanche in July 2003. The interview, mostly done at Shambala game lodge, was in celebration of Nelson Mandela's 85th birthday

on himself

I have always regarded myself, in the first place, as an African patriot.

From the dock at the Rivonia Treason Trial, 20 April 1964. It took him two weeks, working in his cell at night, to write the speech

I don't think there is much history can say about me.

I wanted to be able to stand and fight with my people and to share the hazards of war with them.

From the Rivonia Treason Trial, 20 April 1964

I was made, by the law, a criminal, not because of what I had done, but because of what I stood for, because of what I thought, because of my conscience.

Spoken at the Old Synagogue Trial, Pretoria, 7 November 1962

I'm an ordinary person, I have made serious mistakes, I have serious weaknesses.

I am what I am, both as a result of people who respected me and helped me, and of those who did not respect me and treated me badly.

I will pass through this world but once, and I do not want to divert my attention from my task, which is to unite the nation.

Spoken in February 1996 when he was 77 years old

Rather than being an asset, I'm more of a decoration.

Referring to himself as President of South Africa

In prison I had been worried by people depicting me as a superhuman being who could achieve the impossible.

Nelson Mandela, reflecting in 1999 on a long life

People expect me to do more than is humanly possible.

I carry with me the frailties of my age and the fetters of prejudice that are a privilege of my years.

He said this in 1997 in front of the International Olympic Committee, Lausanne, in a fruitless bid to persuade them to bring the Olympics to Cape Town in 2004

I haven't suffered to the same extent other people have whilst I was relaxing in prison.

Any man or institution that tries to rob me of my dignity will lose.

I was not a messiah, but an ordinary man who became a leader because of extraordinary circumstances.

This was a frequent refrain: 'That was one of the things that worried me – to be raised to the position of a semi-god – because then you are no longer a human being.'

I seem to arrive more firmly at the conclusion that my own life struggle has had meaning only because, dimly and perhaps incoherently, it has sought to achieve the supreme objective of ensuring that each, without regard to race, colour, gender or social status, could have the possibility to reach for the skies.

Judge me not on how I have risen, but on how many times I have fallen and risen.

Whatever my wishes might be, I cannot bind future generations to remember me in the particular way I would like.

If you come across as a saint, people can be very discouraged.

He said this in a reflective mood in February 2000

I wanted to be known as Mandela, a man with weaknesses, some of which are fundamental, and a man who is committed, but, nevertheless, sometimes fails to live up to expectations.

August 2004

---

on history

History shows that penalties do not deter men when their conscience is aroused.

Ordinary South Africans are determined that the past be known, the better to ensure that it is not repeated.

From a speech launching the Truth and Reconciliation Commission in February 1996

Blaming things on the past does not make them better.

The past is a rich resource on which we can draw in order to make decisions for the future.

PSS

The purpose of studying history is not to deride human action, nor to weep over it or to hate it, but to understand it – and then to learn from it as we contemplate our future.

It is the dictate of history to bring to the fore the kind of leaders who seize the moment, who cohere the wishes and aspirations of the oppressed.

He could have been speaking about himself; he was, in fact, speaking about the murdered black consciousness leader, Steve Bantu Biko, on the commemoration of the 20th anniversary of his death (1997)

---

on home

I long to see the little stones on which I played as a child, the little rivers, where I swam – but I am stationed in Johannesburg.

Spoken with longing just after his release in 1990. When Nelson Mandela built his house in the village of Qunu, Transkei, where he was brought up, he built the house identically to the one he had lived in at Victor Verster Prison, Paarl. He says he 'became friendly with the walls of the house'. To this day, he says he was happiest there, between the years 1988 and 1990

Everybody comes back to where they were born.

He was spending Christmas 1996 at Qunu

It becomes important, the older you get, to return to places where you have wonderful recollections.

For the years of his imprisonment, it was the modest Sowetan house he shared with his then wife, Winnie – No 8115, Orlando West – which he dreamt about. In May 1997, together with

his third wife, Graça Machel, he bought a new
home in Houghton, Johannesburg, specifically
to make space for his 21 grandchildren, some of
whom live with him for extended periods

on homosexuality

There was a time when I reacted with revulsion
against the whole system of being gay.

I was ashamed of my initial views, coming from
a society which did not know this type of thing.

I understand their position, and I think they are
entitled to carry on with what pleases them.

on honour

Which man of honour will desert a lifelong friend
at the insistence of a common opponent and still
retain a measure of credibility with his people?

From an open letter to PW Botha, State
President of South Africa, March 1989, who
had offered him a conditional freedom. Mandela's
youngest daughter, Zindzi, read it to a rapt crowd
at the Jabulani Stadium, Soweto, on 10 February
1985

on his hopes

As I sit in Qunu and grow as ancient as its hills, I will continue to entertain the hope that there has emerged a cadre of leaders in my own country and region, on my continent and in the world, which will not allow that any should be denied their freedom, as we were, that any should be turned into refugees, as we were, that any should be condemned to go hungry, as we were, that any should be stripped of their human dignity, as we were.

He was speaking, for the last time as South African Head of State, to the United Nations' General Assembly, New York, 21 September 1998

on housing

Every man should have a house near where he was born.

He said this to Richard Stengel, who worked with him on Long Walk to Freedom *in April 1993, when he visited the modest house he built himself in the Transkei*

A man is not a man until he has a house of his own.

*Nelson Mandela now has several houses: one
is in Houghton, Johannesburg, which he shares
with his wife, Graça Machel, as he does their
home in Maputo, Mozambique; he has a home
in Cape Town, and one is in Qunu, South Africa,
the village where he spent his childhood. The
Qunu house has been considerably enlarged to
accommodate Nelson Mandela's large family and
friends*

The families who live in shacks with no running
water, sanitation, and electricity are a reminder
that the past continues to haunt the present. $PS1$

on humanity

Many of us will have to pass through the valley
of the shadow of death again and again before we
reach the mountaintops of our desires.

*This was a powerful sentence in Nelson
Mandela's seminal 'No Easy Walk to Freedom'
speech, delivered in September 1953*

It is a fact of the human condition that each shall,
like a meteor – a mere brief passing moment in
time and space – flit across the human stage and
pass out of existence.

*From his Address to the Joint Session of the
Houses of Congress of the USA, 26 June 1990,*

*where he was rapturously received only months
after his release*

To deny any person their human rights is to challenge their very humanity.

Let the strivings of us all prove Martin Luther King Jnr to have been correct when he said that humanity can no longer be tragically bound to the starless midnight of racism and war.

The key to the protection of any minority is to put core civil and political rights beyond the reach of temporary majorities by guaranteeing them as fundamental human rights, enshrined in a democratic constitution.

None of us can be described as having virtues or qualities that raise him or her above others.

After climbing a great hill, one only finds that there are many more hills to climb.

The universe we inhabit as human beings is becoming a common home that shows growing disrespect for the rigidities imposed on humanity by national boundaries.

Deep down in every human heart, there is mercy and generosity.

As long as poverty, injustice and gross inequality persist in our world, none of us can truly rest.

on imperialism

> **Imperialism means the denial** of political and economic rights and the perpetual subjugation of the people by a foreign power.
>
> **Imperialism has been weighed** and found wanting.

on being impetuous

It's very important not to shoot from the hip.

on important things

The important thing is to give happiness to people.

Nelson Mandela said this in a television interview to mark his 85th birthday (and the fifth anniversary of his marriage to Graça Machel)

on Inauguration Day, 10 May 1994

One of the outstanding human victories of the century.

I was overwhelmed with a sense of history.

The time for the healing of the wounds has come. The moment to bridge the chasms that divide us has come. The time to build is upon us.

Taken from his Inaugural speech. His inauguration as President of South Africa was held at the Union Buildings in Pretoria, a day no South African who watched it will ever forget

on India

India's independence was a victory for all people under colonial rule.

A part of India's soul resides in South Africa as a revered part of our national life.

He was referring to Mahatma Gandhi

on Islam

Islam has enriched and become part of Africa; in turn, Islam was transformed and Africa became part of it.

on jellybeans

What are jellybeans? Are they something that is eaten?

on June 16 (Freedom Day)

June 16 is the day on which we South Africans commemorate the contribution of our youth to the achievement of democracy, and rededicate ourselves to creating a just society. Celebrated in South Africa as Freedom Day, June 16 1976 was the day on which the youth of Soweto rose in anger against the use of Afrikaans in schools. This escalated into what is known as the Soweto Uprising. It led directly to the end of apartheid and to the exile of many thousands of young South Africans who left the country illegally to join resistance movements such as the ANC.

on justice

In our country and throughout the British world, as far as I know, and in the jurisprudence of many civilised countries, a person is regarded as innocent until he is convicted.

on his last day

On my last day I want to know that those who remain behind will say: 'The man who lies here has done his duty for his country and his people.'
On being welcomed home to Qunu on his
retirement in 1999

on leadership

It is a mistake to think that a single individual can unite the country.

When you want to get the cattle to move in a certain direction, you stand at the back with a stick, and then you get a few of the cleverer cattle to go to the front and move in the direction that you want them to go. The rest of the cattle follow the few more energetic cattle in the front, but you are really guiding them from the back.

Nelson Mandela then added: 'That is how a leader should do his work'

I never choose between stars or teams – it's a tactless thing for a leader to do.

Mandela's reasoning was that if you put a team or a star above others you immediately forfeit their support

There are times when a leader can show sorrow, in public, and that it will not diminish him in the eyes of his people.

As when he comforted Nomboniso Gasa, who was raped on Robben Island in January 1997. He openly showed his distress and anger

Many in positions of power and privilege pursue cold-hearted philosophies which terrifyingly proclaim: I am not your brother's keeper!

He was speaking to the United Nations in October 1995

A leadership commits a crime against its own people if it hesitates to sharpen its political weapons which have become less effective.

A leader who relies on authority to solve problems is bound to come to grief.

We have the high salaries and we are living in luxury: that destroys your capacity to speak in a forthright manner and tell people to tighten their belts.

From a September 1994 interview some four months after he was inaugurated as President of South Africa

It is important to surround yourself with strong and independent personalities, who will tell you when you are getting old.

Nelson Mandela said this in 1996 when there was speculation about his health, and queries were being raised in South Africa as to whether he would be able to complete his term of office

It is the fate of leadership to be misunderstood; for historians, academics, writers and journalists to reflect great lives according to their own subjective canon.

 The mark of great leaders is the ability to understand the context in which they are operating and act accordingly.

---

on liberation

The people are their own liberators.

---

on Libya

The people of Libya shared the trenches with us in our struggle for freedom.

This was said at a banquet in Tripoli, Libya, in October 1997. Nelson Mandela went to great lengths to get to the pariah country, and was staunch – and even angry – in the face of American disapproval. One of his mottoes is never to forget a friend – even if they are held in opprobrium by many

---

on life

Life is like a big wheel: the one who's at the top, tomorrow is at the bottom.

on literature

We could not have made an acquaintance through literature with human giants such as George Washington, Abraham Lincoln and Thomas Jefferson and not been moved to act as they were moved to act.

He said this in a speech to the US Congress in June 1990, shortly after his release from incarceration. One of Nelson Mandela's favourite poems was William Ernest Henley's Invictus; Irish poet Seamus Heaney's work was also important to him, and he has quoted South African poet Ingrid Jonker on several occasions

When we read we are able to travel to many places, meet many people and understand the world.

Whilst on Robben Island, Mandela and his fellow prisoners avidly read Shakespeare: Coriolanus, Henry V and Julius Caesar being favourites. The prisoners staged Sophocles' Antigone, in which Mandela played the part of the tyrant Creon

on longevity

If your attitude is to do things which are going to please the community and human beings, then of course you are likely to live a long life. To go to bed feeling that you have done some service to the community is very important.

---

on love

The world is truly round and seems to start and end with those we love.

From a letter to Winnie, 1 July 1979

I am not nervous of love for love is very inspiring.

Spoken on his State visit to the UK, July 1996.
Only a few people at that time knew of his love
for Graça Machel, widow of Samora Machel,
President of Mozambique

To be in love is an experience that every man must go through.

One should be so grateful at being involved in such an experience.

It is such a wonderful period for me.

Spoken in April 1997, and referring to his
relationship with Graça Machel

I'm in love with a remarkable lady. She has changed my life.

This was said with a broad smile in a South
African television interview in February 1998.
The remarkable lady was, of course, Graça

Machel, whom he married on his 80th birthday,
18 July 1998

I don't regret the setbacks I have had before and,
late in my life, I am blooming like a flower because
of her support.

Again, referring to Graça Machel

Holding Graça's hand is the one thing I love most
in the world.

People must learn to hate, and if they can learn
to hate, they can be taught to love, for love comes
more naturally to the human heart than its
opposite.

first experiences are of love (Mom & Dad)

on marriage

The whole purpose of a husband and wife is that
when hard times knock at the door you should be
able to embrace each other.

According to our custom, you marry the village
and not the human being.

A man and wife usually discuss their most intimate problems in the bedroom.

Spoken in March 1996, in public, at his divorce
hearing from his second wife, Winnie

Ladies don't want to be marrying an old man like me.

On being asked towards the end of 1996 whether he would marry Graça Machel

---

his marriage to Graça Machel, 18 July 1998

Now you won't shout at me and say I am setting a bad example.

Nelson Mandela said this to fellow Nobel Peace Prize holder, Archbishop Desmond Tutu, immediately after his marriage. Tutu had criticised him for living with Graça and setting a bad example

My wife has put a spring in me and made me full of hope.

He said this in May 2002 after nearly four years of marriage to Graça

---

Evelyn Mase, his first wife

She was a quiet, pretty girl from the countryside who did not seem over-awed by the comings and goings.

*He met his first wife in the lounge of Walter
and Albertina Sisulu's home. He asked her to
marry him within a few months and married in
a civil ceremony at the Native Commissioner's
Court in Johannesburg. They had four children
(Thembikile, 1946; Makaziwe, 1947, who
died at nine months; Makgatho, 1951; and
Makaziwe, 1954) and divorced in 1958*

Winnie Madikizela-Mandela, his second wife

She was dazzling, and even the fact that she had
never before tasted curry and drank glass after
glass of water to cool her palate only added to her
charm.

*The couple's first date was at an Indian
restaurant near his Johannesburg offices. He says
he asked her to marry him on their first date,
but Winnie always claimed he didn't propose to
her at all. They were married in a local church* 3B y⌁
*in Bizana on 14 June 1958 and divorced only in
March 1996. They had two daughters*

I had hoped to build you a refuge, no matter how
small, so that we would have a place for rest and
sustenance before the arrival of the sad, dry days.

*From a letter to Winnie from Robben Island, 26
June 1977*

Had it not been for your visits, wonderful letters and your love, I would have fallen apart many years ago.

From a letter to Winnie, 6 May 1979

I have often wondered whether any kind of commitment can ever be sufficient excuse for abandoning a young and inexperienced woman in a pitiless desert.

Letter to Winnie after her 1986 'Boxes and Matches' speech

I cannot say for certain if there is such a thing as love at first sight, but I do know that the moment I first glimpsed Winnie Nomzamo, I knew that I wanted to have her as my wife.

She married a man who soon left her; that man became a myth; and then that myth returned home and proved to be just a man after all.

In a curiously similar turn of phrase, Graça Machel, widow of President Samora Machel of Mozambique, and Nelson Mandela's third wife, said of him in an interview at the beginning of 1998: 'I found this very simple man who appeared so humble, so soft, so common. It was a conflict between myth and the reality.'

I embrace her with all the love and affection I have nursed for her inside and outside prison from the moment I first met her.

Announcing his separation from Winnie,
13 April 1992

My love for her remains undiminished.

Part of his poignant separation announcement

I was the loneliest man during the period I stayed
with her.

During his divorce trial, March 1996

on memory

In the life of any individual, family, community or
society, memory is of fundamental importance.

Memory is the fabric of identity.

At the heart of every oppressive tool developed
by the apartheid regime was a determination
to control, distort, weaken, even erase people's
memories.

on men

Men must follow the dictates of their conscience
irrespective of the consequences which might
overtake them for it.

This was part of his 'Black Man in a White
Court' statement in the Old Synagogue, Pretoria,

on 15 October 1962. The Rivonia Treason Trial
still lay ahead

---

on the Middle East peace process

The spurning of agreements reached in good faith
and the forceful occupation of land can only fan
the flames of conflict.

Extremists on all sides thrive, fed by the blood lust
of centuries gone by.

Palestinian and Israeli campaigners for peace
know that security for any nation is not abstract;
neither is it exclusive.

At the end of a century which has seen a desert
of devastation caused by horrific wars, a century
which has at last gained much experience in the
peaceful resolution of conflicts, we must ask: is
this a time for war; is this a time for sending young
men to their death?

This was said on his being awarded an Honorary
Doctorate by Ben-Gurion University of the
Negev, 19 September 1997

on misfortunes

There are few misfortunes in this world that you cannot turn into a personal triumph if you have the iron will and the necessary skill.

on morality

A movement without a vision is a movement without moral foundation.

on the National Party

We are hopeful that, in their role, they will add another brick into the edifice of our young democracy.

Nelson Mandela was speaking in parliament in June 1996

For people that had to invoke the name of God as they made our people suffer? For people who warped the concept of Christianity to cloak the abomination of apartheid in it?

He was incredulously referring to the National Party, the bulwark of apartheid until 1994, versus the South African Communist Party

on negotiation

Concessions are inherent in negotiations.

When you negotiate you have to accept the integrity of another man.

When you negotiate you must be prepared to compromise.

Negotiated solutions can be found even to conflicts that have come to seem intractable and that such solutions emerge when those who have been divided reach out to find the common ground.

Only free men can negotiate.

He wrote this in a letter to then State President PW Botha, dismissing with contempt Botha's offer of conditional release. And although it was illegal for Mandela's words to be repeated in *South Africa at that time, his letter was defiantly read out to the crowds by his youngest daughter, Zindzi, at Jabulani Stadium, Soweto, on 10 February 1985. He had another five years of imprisonment to go*

If successful negotiations lead to talk of miracles, then it is in part because they achieve what pain too long endured had made to seem impossible.

This was part of a lecture he gave at Trinity College, Dublin, in April 2000

on the new world order

Can we say with confidence that it is within our reach to declare that never again shall continents, countries or communities be reduced to the smoking battlefields of contending forces of nationality, religion, race or language?

Intervention only works when the people concerned seem to be keen for peace.

If I have any moral authority – and I say if – moral authority doesn't solve world problems.

The reality can no longer be ignored that we live in an interdependent world which is bound together to a common destiny.

As the world frees itself from the dominance of bi-polar power the stark division of the world's people into rich and poor comes all the more clearly into view.

We operate in a world which is searching for a better life – without the imprisonment of dogma.

Let us join hands to ensure that as we enter the new millennium, the political rights that the twentieth century has recognised, and the independence that nations have gained, shall be translated into peace, prosperity and equity for all.

As consciousness grows about the inter-depen-
dence of the nations on our planet, so do all major
decisions that derive from the system of governance become subject to international review and
become dependent for their success on approval
and support by an international constituency.

As the process of globalisation grows apace, so
does the system of international governance also
grow stronger.

The problems are such that for anybody with a
conscience who can use whatever influence he
may have to try to bring about peace, it's difficult
to say no.

He was asked if, in spite of his retirement,
he would help to bring about peace in Iraq
(September 2002)

---

on the Nobel Peace Prize

Let it never be said by future generations that
indifference, cynicism or selfishness made us fail
to live up to the ideals of humanism which the
Nobel Peace Prize encapsulates.

Nobel Peace Prize ceremony, Norway,
10 December 1993. He received the award
jointly with FW de Klerk, at that time still State
President of South Africa. The Nobel Peace Prize
had a special meaning for him, because his award

*was preceded by two other South Africans: Chief
Albert Luthuli, former president of the ANC was
a Nobel Peace Prize winner, as was Archbishop
Desmond Tutu*

I assumed the Nobel Committee would never con-
sider for the peace prize the man who had started
Umkhonto we Sizwe.

*Spear of the Nation, the military wing of the
ANC, formed by Nelson Mandela in June 1961.
Arguing his case, he said: 'Sebatana ha se bokwe
ka diatla.' ('The attacks of the wild beast cannot
be averted with only bare hands.')*

---

on old ANC comrades

In the last few years we have walked this road with
greater frequency, marching in the procession to
bid farewell to the veterans of our movement,
paying our last respects to the fallen spears of the
nation from a generation now reaching the end of
a long and heroic struggle.

*He was speaking at the funeral of his friend of
60 years, the self-effacing Walter Sisulu (May
2003).*

Those of us from that generation, who are singled
out to stay the longest, have to bear the pain of
seeing our comrades go.

They fought a noble battle and lived their lives in pursuit of a better life for all who follow.

The democracy in which we bury them and honour them is the sweet fruit of their lives of struggle and sacrifice.

on Olympians

The difference between Olympians and the rest of us is: they behave as long-time friends who occasionally compete, while we behave as long-time adversaries who occasionally get along.

on oppression

To overthrow oppression has been sanctioned by humanity and is the highest aspiration of every free man.

From his famous 'No Easy Walk to Freedom'
speech, 1954

For as long as legitimate bodies of opinion feel stifled, vile minds will take advantage of justifiable grievances to destroy, to kill and to maim.

For as long as the majority of people anywhere on the continent [of Africa] feel oppressed, are not allowed democratic participation in decision-making process, and cannot elect their own leaders in free and fair elections, there will always be tension and conflict.

Never and never again shall the laws of our land rend our people apart or legalise their oppression and repression.

---

on Orania

The way in which we were received by everybody in Orania was as if I was in Soweto.

Nelson Mandela visited the diehard all-white dorp of Orania in the Northern Cape to visit the 94-year-old widow of the architect of apartheid, Hendrik Verwoerd(August 1995). When she died at 98 he noted that 'She and her husband are part of South Africa's history even though we sharply condemned their policies.'

---

on the Organisation of African Unity (OAU)

[It is] the midwife of our freedom.

Nelson Mandela made this comment towards the end of his presidency. He was speaking at the Summit Meeting of OAU Heads of State and Government, Ouagadougou, Burkina Faso, 8 June 1998

on his parents

My father was a polygamist with four wives and nine children.

My mother was my first friend in the proper sense of the word.

The graves mean a great deal to me because my beloved parents are here and it arouses a great deal of emotion in me because part of myself lies buried here.

He was standing next to his parents' simple graves in Qunu. His mother died while he was on Robben Island and the authorities denied him permission to attend her funeral. The first time he was able to pay his respects to her was after his release from prison in 1990

on peace

Peace and democracy go hand in hand.

It is not easy to talk about peace to people who are mourning every day.

I will go down on my knees to beg those who want to drag our country into bloodshed and persuade them not to do so.

Peace and prosperity, tranquillity and security are only possible if these are enjoyed by all without discrimination.

We live in a world and in times in which it is recognized that peace is the most powerful weapon any community or people has to bring about stability and progress through development.

This was part of the Independent News and Media lecture he delivered at Trinity College, Dublin, in April 2000

on people

I love you. You are my own flesh and blood. You are my brothers, sisters, children and grandchildren.

Speaking to the people of South Africa

I surely wish the pockets of my shirt were big enough to fit all of you in.

To his compatriots in the Transkei

Language, culture and religion are important indicators of identity.

Justice and liberty must be our tool, prosperity and happiness our weapon.

It is in the character of growth that we should learn from both pleasant and unpleasant experiences.

The suffering of the people of any single country affects all of us no matter where we find ourselves.

[I am] an old man who loves you all from the bottom of his heart.

You must accept the integrity of everyone and let bygones be bygones.

---

on personalities

Steve Biko, murdered black consciousness activist

There can be no doubt that he was one of the most talented and colourful freedom fighters South Africa has produced.

[He was] one of the greatest sons of our nation.

He said this in East London on 12 September 1997, the 20th anniversary of Steve Biko's death

That he was indeed a great man who stood head and shoulders above his peers is borne out not only by the testimony of those who knew him and worked with him, but by the fruit of his endeavours.

A fitting product of his time; a proud representative of the re-awakening of a people.

George Bush, former president of the USA

I am aware that he is surrounded by dinosaurs who offer him all sorts of advice.

He said this as US war drums were attempting to muster support for unilateral action against Iraq, September 2002. He further separated Bush from the actions of his administration by describing Deputy President Dick Cheney as 'an arch-conservative' and George Bush as 'a man with whom you can do business.'

Mangosuthu Buthelezi, IFP president and politician

When we are together, he is very, very courteous. But when he is away from you, he behaves totally differently, because he does not know if he is still your friend or not.

The problem is when he leaves the cabinet and appears on public platforms. Then he behaves like any other politician.

Prince Charles

This is a real king, not the Lion King.

Nelson Mandela's grandchildren were being
introduced to Prince Charles during his historic
official visit to South Africa, October 1997. The
Prince of Wales was accompanied by his younger
son, Prince Harry

Bill Clinton, former US president

There is a vow of goodwill between us.

President Clinton has been my friend even before
he became president. I respect him very much.

I will support my friend even if he has been
deserted by the entire world.

He said this at a press conference in Washington
on his last official visit to the USA as President
of South Africa, September 1998

Hansie Cronje, disgraced captain of the Proteas

I am saying without excusing what he has done
if the allegations are proven right, that he can be
a role model and turn this tragedy into triumph.

*Alas, in his confession to evangelist Ray
McCauley, placed before the King Commission
of Inquiry in 2002, Hansie said: 'In a moment
of stupidity and weakness, I allowed Satan and
the world to dictate terms to me, rather than the
Lord.'*

His untimely death is one of those pieces of
human tragedy that leaves us so shocked.

*Hansie Cronje was killed in a plane crash on 1
June 2002*

FW de Klerk, former state president

He had the courage to admit that a terrible wrong
had been done to our country and people through
the imposition of the system of apartheid.

Nobel Peace Prize Address

If there is anything that has cooled relations
between me and Mr de Klerk, it is his paralysis as
far as violence is concerned.

*This was said in September 1992, with reference
to the Boipatong massacre and the increasingly
inexplicable 'third force' violence in South Africa*

Dis goed om te sien hoe ons saam oud word (It's
good to see us growing old together).

*Nelson Mandela at FW de Klerk's 70th birthday
party on 17 March 2006, Three South African*

*Nobel Peace Laureates were at the party, held
at the Mount Nelson, Cape Town: De Klerk,
Mandela and Desmond Tutu*

Diana, Princess of Wales

I found her very graceful, highly intelligent, and
committed to worthy causes, and I was tremen-
dously impressed by her warmness.

[She] became a citizen of the world through her
care for people everywhere.

*He said this at the State Banquet for Prince
Charles held in Cape Town, South Africa, on 4
November 1997*

Queen Elizabeth II

The Queen is a very gracious lady and I'm sure
she'll put a country boy at ease.

*On the eve of his historic – and jubilant – state
visit to Britain, July 1996*

Muammar Gaddafi, president of Libya

He helped us at a time when we were all alone, when those who are now saying we should not come here were helping our enemies.

Said at the start of his controversial October 1997 visit to Libya, in the face of UN and US disapproval

My brother leader.

Mahatma Gandhi

It would not be right to compare me to Gandhi. None of us could equal his dedication or his humility.

He showed us that it was necessary to brave imprisonment if truth and justice were to triumph over evil.

Nelson Mandela was speaking at the conferral of the Freedom of Pietermaritzburg on Mahatma Gandhi in April 1997

We must never lose sight of the fact that the Gandhian philosophy may be a key to human survival in the twenty-first century.

Opening of the Gandhi Hall, Lenasia
27 September 1992

Chris Hani, assassinated leader of the South African Communist Party

A white man, full of prejudice and hate, came to our country and committed a deed so foul that our whole nation now teeters on the brink of disaster. A white woman, of Afrikaner origin, risked her life so that we might know, and bring to justice, this assassin.

Speech to all South Africans, calming the angry youth after Hani's assassination at the hands of a white man (10 April 1993) The 'white woman' was Hani's neighbour, who witnessed the murder, and alerted the police

---

Archbishop Trevor Huddleston

His sacrifices for our freedom told us that the true relationship between our people was not one between poor citizens on the one hand and good patricians on the other, but one underwritten by our common humanity and our human capacity to touch one another's hearts across the oceans.

Ernest Urban Trevor Huddleston died in Britain in 1998 at the age of 84. At his request, his

ashes were brought back to South Africa, to lie in
his old church in the razed suburb of Sophiatown
where he worked and lived as an Anglican priest
in the 1950s. Joint Houses of Parliament speech
11 July 1996

Michael Jackson, entertainer

He will be missed and memories cherished of him
for a long time. Be strong.

Jackson died at 2.26 pm in Los Angeles on 25
June 2009.

Tony Leon, former Leader of the Opposition, South Africa

[He is] a leader whose dynamism and capacity for
analysis keeps everyone on their toes.

You have far more support for all that you have
done than you might read about.

Nelson Mandela in December 2006, after the
Democratic Alliance leader announced he would
be standing down

Martin Luther King, Jnr

He grappled with and died in the effort to make a contribution to the just solution of the same great issues of the day which we have had to face as South Africans.

From his Nobel Peace Prize Address, 10 December 1993

Patricia de Lille, politician

Patricia de Lille is one of that rare breed of politician of whom it can be said that no matter what political party she would belong to, one cannot help liking and admiring her.

Thabo Mbeki, former President of South Africa

He is polite but he is not a yes-man. He will always stand his ground.

He is a man of exceptional quality, very respectful, very warm.

He was speaking in December 1997

He is a modest man and I know he would prefer that I do not sing his personal praises, but his achievement as president and national leader is the embodiment of what our nation is capable of.

Nelson Mandela addressing the joint session of the two houses of parliament on 10 May 2004 and celebrating a decade of democracy in the country

Whether I'm alive or gone, he will respect the constitution.

Nelson Mandela, during his 85th birthday celebrations in 2003

Robert Mugabe, politician

[There has been] a tragic failure of leadership in our neighbouring Zimbabwe.

Mandela has always been discreet regarding his northern neighbour. In a brief but pointed speech at a dinner for his 90th birthday in London he mentioned not only Robert Mugabe but Darfur ('We watch with sadness the continuing tragedy in Darfur')

Beyers Naude, cleric

He inspired us – that's the value of Oom Bey.

Nelson Mandela, after visiting Naudé's 91-year-old widow, Ilse, on 8 September 2004, following her husband's death the previous day

If someone asks me what kind of a person a New South African should be, I will say: 'Take a look at Beyers and his wife Ilse.'

Oom Bey's life was one of contribution, a true humanitarian and a true son of Africa.

General Colin Powell, US politician

I won't wash this hand you have shaken.

It was a mutual admiration session: Colin Powell had just said: 'This is truly a very great honour for me.'

Cyril Ramaphosa, businessman

He is a son to me.

A young man of considerable ability destined to occupy a very important position in our political life.

Anton Rupert, businessman

Mooi loop, Anton.

Anton Rupert died in his sleep on 18 January 2006. He was one of South Africa's greatest philanthropists

---

Walter Sisulu, politician and lifelong friend

We walked side by side through the valley of death, nursing each other's bruises, holding each other up when our steps faltered. And together we were priviledged to savour the taste of freedom.

Nelson Mandela met Walter Sisulu in 1941. Sisulu, who died in 2003, was a singular influence on him for the rest of his life. They went to Robben Island together. The release of Sisulu ahead of his old friend was a sure sign that the unthinkable was about to happen: the release of Nelson Mandela from prison

While many of us have been honoured by countries in every continent with awards, including Nobel peace prizes, there is one man who has not received some of these, but nonetheless he stands head and shoulders above us all because of his humility and simplicity.

Nelson Mandela, in the foreword to the biography of Walter and Albertina Sisulu In Our Lifetime *by Elinor Sisulu*

I now know that when my time comes, Walter will be there to meet me, and I am almost certain he will hold out an enrolment form to register me into the ANC in that world, cajoling me with one of his favourite songs we sang when mobilizing people behind the Freedom Charter:

*Libhaliwe ma oGama lakho kuloMqulu weNkululeko
Vuma silibhale kuloMqulu weNkululeko.*

(Has your name been enrolled in the struggle for freedom
Permit us to register you in the struggle for freedom.)

*Nelson Mandela, in a statement to SAPA late
at night on 5 May 2003. His dearest friend,
Walter Sisulu, had just died*

Xhamela is no more. May he live forever. His absence has carved a void. A part of me is gone.

From the moment we first met, he has been my friend, my brother, my keeper, my comrade.

*Nelson Mandela, from a tribute he wrote and
which was published on 7 May 2003*

In a sense I feel cheated by Walter. If there be another life beyond this physical world, I would have loved to be there first so that I could welcome him. Life has determined otherwise.

'Don't get involved with that man Walter Sisulu,' I was warned when I first arrived in Johannesburg.

'If you do, you will end up spending the rest of your life in jail.' Of course, I ignored this advice.

Those of us from that generation, who are singled out to stay the longest, have to bear the pain of seeing our comrades go.

How can we speak about this great unifier to people without recognizing and honouring that great unity in his own life: that of Walter and Albertina as a marital couple, a unity of such deep friendship and mutual respect, a personal and political partnership that transcended and survived all hardships, separations and persecution.

He knew how to throw a left hook, but never below the belt.

Nelson Mandela, at the unveiling of the
tombstone of his old friend in December 2003

Adelaide Tambo

A life dedicated to service and freedom.

He had been asked to describe Adelaide Tambo's
life. She died of a heart attack on 1 February
2007, 14 years after her husband, Oliver. She
was 77

Oliver Tambo, former President of the ANC

When I looked at him in his coffin, it was as if a part of myself had died.

Oliver Tambo was Nelson Mandela's lifelong friend. They were in law practice together. Later on the head of the ANC, Tambo lived most of his life in exile. He returned to South Africa, but died shortly afterwards, not living long enough to see his dream of a democratic South Africa realised

He is my greatest friend and comrade for 50 years.

I am not prepared to sell the birthright of the People – open letter to PW Botha, read by Zindzi at Jabulani Stadium, 10 February 1985

He enriched my own life and intellect, and neither I nor indeed this country (South Africa) can forget this colossus of our history.

Address to the closing session of the 50th National Conference of the ANC, Mafikeng 20 December 1997

Nobel Laureate Archbishop Desmond Tutu

He's a terrific fellow.

He has been a blessing and inspiration to countless people through his ministry; his acts of compassion; his prophetic witness; and his political engagement.

Said at the thanksgiving service for the ministry of Archbishop Tutu in Cape Town, June 1996

Jacob Zuma, politician and President of South Africa, May 2009

We wish him well as he considers his future and want to reassure him of our continued friendship.

While we are naturally deeply saddened that a person who had made such a major contribution to our liberation and democracy had to come to this point in his life and career, we fully support the president in this difficult time in the life of our government, nation and organisation.

Nelson Mandela in a statement which supported former President Thabo Mbeki's sacking of Jacob Zuma from his position of Deputy President in June 2005. Later, Zuma resigned as an MP

on his statue, Parliament Square, London

When Oliver Tambo and I visited Westminster Abbey and Parliament Square in 1962, we half-joked that we hoped that one day a statue of a black person would be erected here alongside General Smuts. Oliver would have been proud today.

Nelson Mandela after his statue was unveiled

The history of the struggle in South Africa is rich with the story of heroes and heroines, some of them leaders, some of them followers. All of them deserve to be remembered.

Nelson Mandela, in Parliament Square, London, 29 August 2007, after his 2.7m bronze statue was unveiled, making him the second South African, after Jan Smuts, to be given the rare recognition of a place opposite the Houses of Parliament. British Prime Minister Gordon Brown, in his speech, said: 'From this day forward, this statue will stand here, in sight of this ancient forum of democracy, to commemorate and celebrate for the ages triumph in the greatest of causes and the most inspiring and greatest leader of our generation – and one of the most courageous and best-loved men of all time.'

Though this statue is of one man, in actual fact it symbolises all those who have resisted oppression, especially in my country.

---

on the art of persuasion

Don't address their brains. Address their hearts.

---

on stealing pigs

We had a method as young chaps of about 16 or 17 of stealing pigs. We had very clever ways of doing so. We would take the remains of kaffir beer, as they called it, and then we'd go to the direction of the wind, so that the wind would blow it from us to the village where the pigs were. And then we'd leave a little bit of the remains of the beer, and then the pigs come out ... Then we put the stuff further away ... and they will follow us. When they are far away ... we stab it ... the owners will not hear its shouts, and then we roast it and eat it.

Nelson Mandela was talking with the Oscar-winning Tsotsi *stars Presley Chweneyagae, Terry Pheto and director Gavin Hood after they returned triumphantly from Hollywood in March 2006*

on photography

Good use of photography will give even poverty with all its rags, filth and vermin a measure of divineness rarely noticeable in real life.

Letter to his daughter Zindzi, 6 August 1979

on politics

Political division, based on colour, is entirely artificial and, when it disappears, so will the domination of one colour group by another.

From the dock at the Rivonia Treason Trial, 20 April 1964

We should not allow South African politics to be relegated to trivialities chosen precisely because they salve the consciences of the rich and powerful, and conceal the plight of the poor and powerless.

75th anniversary of the SACP, 28 July 1996

If you are a politician you must be prepared to suffer for your principles.

on poverty

It should never be that the anger of the poor should be the finger of accusation pointed at all of us because we failed to respond to the cries of the people for food, for shelter, for the dignity of the individual.

Address to US Congress, 28 June 1990

We can neither heal nor build, if on the one hand, the rich in our society see the poor as hordes of irritants; or if, on the other hand, the poor sit back, expecting charity.

None can be at peace while others wallow in poverty and insecurity.

International Day of Solidarity with the Palestinians, 4 December 1997

Poverty still grips our people. If you're poor, you're not likely to live for long.

Said in a 90th birthday interview with CNN

Poverty and deprivation in our midst demean all of us.

This was part of a short speech made at the ANC rally at Loftus Versfeld, Pretoria, to celebrate his 90th birthday in July 2008

In this new century, millions of people in the world's poorest countries remain imprisoned, enslaved and in chains. They are trapped in the prison of poverty. It is time to set them free.

He was speaking to an audience of thousands in Trafalgar Square, London, on 3 February 2005, the eve of a meeting by the finance ministers of the Group of Seven industrialised nations. When he heard after he became President of South Africa in May 1994 what his salary would be (R700 000pa) he said: 'No, this is too high. I would like you to cut it down', which was promptly done

Poverty is man-made and can be overcome and eradicated by the actions of human beings.

on praise

I think the accolades that one gets are more because of old age.

He was 80 when he said this

on being president (of South Africa)

This has placed a great responsibility on my shoulders.

We enter into a covenant that we shall build a society in which all South Africans, both black and white, will be able to walk tall, without any fear in their hearts, assured of their inalienable right to human dignity – a rainbow nation at peace with itself and the world.

From his Inaugural speech, 10 May 1994

At the end of my term I'll be 81. I don't think it's wise that a robust country like South Africa should be led by a septuagenarian.

Spoken in 1996 when there were rumours about his health

It is a way of life in which it's hard to dedicate time to the things that are really close to your heart.

My present life, even if it's not the easiest way of life, is very rewarding.

Spoken in mid-1997, one of his busiest years

on the press

A critical, independent and investigative press is the lifeblood of any democracy.

It was the press who never forgot us.

Spoken just after his February 1990 release

A press conference is not a place to discuss rumours.

The press is one of the pillars of democracy.

A bad free press is preferable to a technically good, subservient one.

None of our irritations with the perceived inadequacies of the media should ever allow us to suggest even faintly that the independence of the press could be compromised or coerced.

---

on **prison**

Nothing is more dehumanising than isolation from human companionship.

Nelson Mandela saw Robben Island for the first time from Table Mountain, Cape Town, in 1947. Less than 20 years later, he was incarcerated there

The long, lonely wasted years.

He was prisoner 466/64

I believe the way in which you are treated by the prison authorities depends on your demeanour and you must fight that battle and win it on the very first day.

There I had time, just to sit for hours and think.

The advantage of prison life is that you can sit and think and see yourself and your work from a distance.

In prison I had been worried by people depicting me as a superhuman being who could achieve the impossible.

He was reflecting on a long life in 1999

What always worried me in prison was [that I could acquire] the image of someone who is always 100 per cent correct and can never do any wrong.

He was speaking at the launch of a book about him in November 1999

I realised that they could take it all except my mind and heart. And I just made a decision not to give them away.

Nelson Mandela, as quoted by Bill Clinton in November 2000. Mandela was referring to his jailers and to the people who had put him in prison

on racism

I detest racialism, because I regard it as a barbaric thing, whether it comes from a black man or a white man.

*'Black Man in a White Court' statement, Old
Synagogue, 15 October 1962*

Racism pollutes the atmosphere of human relations and poisons the minds of the backward, the
bigoted and the prejudiced.

Harlem speech, 21 June 1990

Our struggle is the struggle to erase the colour line
that all too often determines who is rich and who
is poor.

Harlem speech, 21 June 1990

As we enter the last decade of the twentieth
century, it is intolerable and unacceptable that the
cancer of racism is still eating away at the fabric of
societies in different parts of our planet.

Harlem speech, 21 June 1990

We must ensure that colour, race and gender
become only a God-given gift to each one of us and
not an indelible mark or attribute that accords a
special status to any.

Address to UN, 3 October 1994

Racism is a blight on the human conscience.

*Joint Houses of Parliament speech, 11 July
1996*

We shall never again allow our country to play
host to racism. Nor shall our voices be stilted if we

see that another, elsewhere in the world, is victim to racial tyranny.

Joint Houses of Parliament speech, 11 July 1996

Racism must be consciously combated and not discreetly tolerated.

Clark University Investiture, 10 July 1993

The very fact that racism degrades both the perpetrator and the victim commands that, if we are true to our commitment to protect human dignity, we fight on until victory is achieved.

Address to UK parliament, 11 July 1996

All of us know how stubbornly racism can cling to the mind and how deeply it can infect the human soul.

Address to UN General Assembly, 3 October 1994

It will perhaps come to be that we who have harboured in our country the worst example of racism since the defeat of Nazism, will make a contribution to human civilisation by ordering our affairs in such a manner that we strike an effective and lasting blow against racism everywhere.

Address to UK parliament, 11 July 1996

I hate the practice of race discrimination, and in my hatred I am sustained by the fact that the overwhelming majority of mankind hate it equally.

'Black Man in a White Court' statement, Old Synagogue, 15 October 1962

Death to racism.

Harlem speech, 21 June 1990

When the secretaries-general [of the UN] were white, we never had the question of any country ignoring the UN. But now that we have black secretaries-general, certain countries that believe in white supremacy are ignoring the UN. We have to combat that without reservation.

Nelson Mandela, in Jakarta, Indonesia, September 2002. He repeated that statement, in regard to the Iraq crisis, in February 2003, when he said: 'Both US President Bush as well as Tony Blair are undermining an idea which was sponsored by their predecessors. Is this because the secretary-general of the UN is now a black man? They never did that when secretaries-general were white.'

Social problems don't just change because you have made a law – it takes a great deal of time.

Nelson Mandela said this in February 2004 when he was presented with an honorary doctorate from Britain's Open University by

the former Speaker of the House of Commons,
Baroness Betty Boothroyd

---

on reaching heaven

I will look for a branch of the ANC and join it.

---

on reconciliation

The mission of reconciliation is underpinned by what I have dedicated my life to: uplifting the most down-trodden sections of our population and all round transformation of society.

Above all the healing process involves the nation, because it is the nation itself that needs to redeem and reconstruct itself.

Interfaith Commissioning Service for the TRC,
13 February 1996

Reconstruction goes hand in hand with reconciliation.

Thanksgiving Service for Archbishop Tutu, 23
June 1996

We can easily be enticed to read reconciliation and fairness as meaning parity between justice and injustice.

International Day of Solidarity with the
Palestinian People, 4 December 1997

on Regina Mundi

A church that refused to allow God's name to be
used to justify discrimination and repression.

Regina Mundi Day, 30 November 1997. Regina
Mundi is a cathedral in Soweto, frequently
the focus of defiance during the struggle, and
symbolic to many of the fight for freedom

A literal battlefield between forces of democracy
and those who did not hesitate to violate a place
of religion with teargas, dogs and guns.

Regina Mundi Day, 30 November 1997

Regina Mundi became a worldwide symbol of the
determination of our people to free themselves.

Regina Mundi Day, 30 November 1997

on regrets

My greatest regret in life is that I never became the
heavyweight boxing champion of the world.

on relaxing

When I have no visitors over weekends, I remain the whole day in my pyjamas and eat samp. ?

You must find your own garden.

For Nelson Mandela, the garden was not a place of retreat but of renewal. His first garden was on Robben Island (there are now no traces of it) although he used to grow enough spinach to feed fellow political prisoners on Sunday after Sunday. When he was transferred to Pollsmoor Prison in 1982, he had an garden using thirty-two, sliced in half, 44-gallon oil drums. According to his biographer, Richard Stengel, he grew tomatoes, onions, aubergines, strawberries, spinach and other vegetables, working on the garden for two hours every morning and again later in the day

on his release from prison

I greet you all in the name of peace, democracy and freedom for all.

Historic words indeed; he said them to the wildly excited crowd as he walked out of Victor Verster Prison, Paarl, holding the hand of his then wife Winnie on 11 February 1990. He was 71

I would be merely rationalising if I told you that I am able to describe my own feelings. It was breathtaking, that is all I can say.

Along the route [from Paarl to Cape Town] I was surprised to see the number of whites who seemed to identify themselves with what is happening to the country today amongst blacks.

I was completely overwhelmed by the enthusiasm.

---

on religion

Without the church, without religious institutions, I would never have been here today.

The simple lesson of religions, of all philosophies and of life itself is that, although evil may be on the rampage temporarily, the good must win the laurels in the end.

From a letter to his friend, Fatima Meer, 1 January 1976. Less than six months later, the Soweto uprising broke out, signalling the eventual end of apartheid

The strength of inter-religious solidarity in action against apartheid, rather than mere harmony or co-existence, was critical in bringing that evil system to an end.

'Renewal & Renaissance – Towards a New World Order'; lecture at the Oxford Centre for Islamic Studies, 11 July 1997

[African traditional religion] is no longer seen as despised superstition which had to be superseded by superior forms of belief; today its enrichment of humanity's spiritual heritage is acknowledged.

'Renewal & Renaissance' lecture at the Oxford Centre for Islamic Studies, 11 July 1997

We need religious institutions to continue to be the conscience of society, a moral custodian and a fearless champion of the interests of the weak and downtrodden.

Regina Mundi Day, 30 November 1997

Whether you are a Christian, a Muslim, a Buddhist, a Jew or a Hindu, religion is a great force and it can help one have command of one's own morality, one's own behaviour and one's own attitude.

on preparing for his retirement

I must step down while there are one or two people who admire me.

November 1996, when he was 77

I intend to do a bit of farming when I step down. I will be without a job and I don't want to find myself standing at the side of the road with a placard saying: unemployed.

There is no reason whatsoever for anyone to think there will be dislocation in South Africa as a result of the stepping down of an individual.

I look forward to the period when I will be able to wake up with the sun, to walk the hills and valleys of Qunu in peace and tranquillity.

Nelson Mandela has often spoken of Qunu with longing. On this occasion it was especially so. This was the final sentence in his 'private' (as opposed to his controversial five-hour 'political') speech at the historic 50th ANC conference held in Mafikeng in December 1997, when he relinquished his presidency of the ANC, and clearly looked ahead towards his retirement in 1999

I will be able to have that opportunity in my last years to spoil my grandchildren and try in various ways to assist all South African children, especially those who have been the hapless victims of a system that did not care.

ANC Conference speech, 20 December 1997

My retirement will give me the opportunity to sit down with my children and grandchildren and

no such luxury when glory is at stake

listen to their dreams and to help them as much
as possible.

I will still go into Shell House on Mondays and
carry out whatever instructions my president
gives me.

*Shell House, the former ANC headquarters, is in
the heart of Johannesburg. The president of the
ANC in December 1997 was Thabo Mbeki*

Born as World War I came to a close and departing
from public life as the world marks half a century
of the Universal Declaration of Human Rights, I
have reached that part of the long walk when the
opportunity is granted, as it should be to all men
and women, to retire to some rest and tranquillity
in the village of my birth.

*Mandela was speaking to the United Nations'
General Assembly in September 1998. It was
his last address as South African head of State.
Many in the audience had tears in their eyes*

It is as a peaceful and equitable world takes shape
that I and the legions across the globe who dedicated their lives in striving for a better life for all
will be able to retire in contentment and at peace.

*Part of his address to the World Council of
Churches, 1998*

I'll get a board that says 'Unemployed' and stand
on street corners.

This was his standard joke for some time before his retirement

I'm a part of the world. I will work with the UN, which does sterling work – if I am needed.

If there's anything that would kill me it is to wake up in the morning not knowing what to do.

He said this in 2002, when he was 84

---

on his retirement as president of the African National Congress (ANC)

The time has come to hand over the baton in a relay that started more than 85 years ago in Mangaung; nay more, centuries ago when the warriors of the Autshumanyo, Makhanda, Mzilikazi, Moshweshwe, Khama, Sekkukkuni, Lobatsibeni, Cetshwayo, Nghunghunyane, Uithalder and Ramabulana, laid down their lives to defend the dignity and integrity of their being as a people.

Here are the reins of the movement – protect and guard its precious legacy.

I will remember this experience fondly for as long as I live.

I know that the love and respect that I have enjoyed is love and respect for the ANC and its ideals.

The time has come for me to take leave.

All the above quotations were taken from Nelson Mandela's valedictory address to the closing session of the historic 50th national conference of the ANC on 20 December 1997. As the speech drew to its conclusion, he had tears in his eyes

---

on his retirement as MP and president of South Africa (1999)

I step down with a clear conscience, feeling that I have in a small way done my duty to my people and my country.

I would like to rest. I welcome the prospect of revelling in obscurity.

I have 27 grandchildren and more are coming ... it tears my heart when I get home and my youngest grandchild asks: 'Grandpa are you going out again?'

Whatever regrets I have are irrelevant.

Nelson Mandela, at a farewell breakfast for the media at the Presidential Guest House, Pretoria, on 10 May 1999

And yet another retirement (2004)

When I told one of my advisers that I wanted to retire, he growled at me. 'You *are* retired'. If that is really the case, then I should say I now announce that I am retiring from retirement.

Mandela was speaking at the offices of the Nelson Mandela Foundation on 1 June 2004. He left a R1 billion endowment to be raised by the three charitable organisations that bear his name (the NelsonMandela Foundation, the Nelson Mandela Children's Fund and the Nelson Mandela Rhodes Foundation), to be used to improve the lives of South Africans

I am confident that nobody present here today will accuse me of selfishness if I ask to spend time, while I am still in good health, with my family, my friends – and also with myself.

I do not intend to hide away totally from the public, but henceforth I want to be in the position of calling you to ask whether I would be welcome, rather than being called upon to do things and participate in events.

The appeal therefore is: don't call me, I'll call you.

At the end of his speech, Mandela received a five minute standing ovation. His response: 'Thank you, it's nice to have billionaires clapping for me.'

on revenge

You can't build a united nation on the basis of revenge.

In an interview with the New York Times in March 1997: he was referring to the Truth and Reconciliation Commission

on the South African right wing

There are still powerful elements among whites who are not reconciled with the present transformation and who want to use every excuse to drown the country in bloodshed.

If you want to mobilise every section of the population, you can't do it with feelings of hatred and revenge.

on Robben Island

Siqithini **– the Island** – a place of pain and banishment for centuries, and now of triumph.

Heritage Day, Robben Island, 24 September 1997

Without question the harshest, most iron-fisted outpost in the South African penal system.

*Robben Island, nine kilometres off the Cape
coast and set in the tumultuous Atlantic Ocean,
has been used as a prison for hundreds of years
– the first prisoner was Harry the Strandloper,
confined there by the Dutch in 1658. But
Robben Island is no longer a prison – it has
been turned into a museum and can be visited
by anyone. Mandela revisited his old prison on
11 February 1994, posing in his old cell in B
Section, and showing the world the limestone
quarry which he and his associates had worked
in year after year*

A symbol of the victory of the human spirit over
political oppression; and of reconciliation over
enforced division.

*Heritage Day, Robben Island, 24 September
1997*

The Island has become a monument of the struggle for democracy, part of a heritage that will
always inspire our children and our friends from
other lands.

*Freedom of the City of Cape Town,
27 November 1997*

---

on Rwanda

Rwanda stands out as a stern and severe rebuke
to all of us.

The louder and more piercing the cries of despair – even when that despair results in half-a-million dead in Rwanda – the more these cries seem to encourage an instinctive reaction to raise our hands so as to close our eyes and ears.

Address to UK parliament, 11 July 1996

None of us can insulate ourselves from so catastrophic a scale of human suffering.

Address to UK parliament, 11 July 1996

---

on the rugby World Cup, South Africa, 1995

Our whole nation stood behind a sport which was once a symbol of apartheid.

None more so than Nelson Mandela himself. He appeared at the final wearing captain Francois Pienaar's No 6 shirt – and brought the entire country along with him, surely one of the most successful efforts at reconciliation in South Africa

When it was 12/12 I almost collapsed. I was absolutely tense.

When I left the stadium my nerves were completely shattered.

I'm still recovering.

In an interview with The New York Times,
1997

And the rugby World Cup, Paris, 2007

You have put us **on the map** of the world because of your performance.

The team visited Nelson Mandela at his Houghton home; coach Jake White and Bok captain John Smit held the Webb Ellis Trophy over Mandela's head in a replay of the 1995 World Cup. And, as in 1995, Mandela was wearing Springbok colours. There was another link with the Rugby World Cup of 1995: Captain John Smit noted shortly after the historic 15-6 Bok win, 'We had 45 million South Africans and the rest of the world shouting for us,' more or less echoing Francois Pienaar's words 12 years before

on sabotage

I planned it as a result of a calm and sober assessment of the situation, after many years of oppression and tyranny of my people by the whites.

From the Rivonia Treason Trial, 20 April 1964 – the trial which sent him to prison for 27 years

on self-respect

If you are in harmony with yourself, you may meet a lion without fear, because he respects anyone with self-confidence.

on soccer

Soccer is one of the sporting disciplines in which Africa is rising to demonstrate her excellence, for too long latent in her womb.

African Cup of Nations Tournament opening,
January 1996

on society

The great lesson of our time is that no regime can survive if it acts above the heads of the ordinary citizens of the country.

A society that does not value its older people denies its roots and endangers its future.

At the launch of the SA leg of the International
Year of Older Persons

Social problems don't just change because you have made a law – it takes a great deal of time.

*Nelson Mandela said this in February 2004
when he was presented with an honorary
doctorate from Britain's Open University by
the former Speaker of the House of Commons,
Baroness Betty Boothroyd*

on South Africa

We are marching to a new future based on a sound
basis of respect.

It is in the deep interests of our country to ensure
that the same principles of freedom and democracy that we hold to be true find resonance in
other parts of the world.

*Chris Hani Award, 10th National Congress of
the SACP, Johannesburg, 1 July 1998*

We live with the hope that as she battles to remake
herself, South Africa will be like a microcosm of
the new world that is striving to be born.

*From his Nobel Peace Prize Address,
10 December 1993*

Each time one of us touches the soil of this land,
we feel a sense of personal renewal.

Inaugural speech, 10 May 1994

Never and never again shall it be that this beautiful land will again experience the oppression of

one by another and suffer the indignity of being
the skunk of the world.

*From his moving Inaugural speech, 10 May
1994*

No society emerging out of the grand disaster of
the apartheid system could avoid carrying the
blemishes of its past.

*Address to Joint Houses of Parliament,
11 July 1996*

If we are able today to speak proudly of a 'rainbow
nation', it is in part because the world set us a
moral example which we dared to follow.

Had the new South Africa emerged out of nothing,
it would not exist.

*Address to Joint Houses of Parliament,
11 July 1996*

The first founding stone of our new country is
national reconciliation and national unity. The
fact that it has settled in its mortar needs no
advertising.

Address to UK parliament, 11 July 1997

We do face major challenges, but none are as
daunting as those we have already surmounted.

*On receiving the Freedom of the City of London,
July 1996*

Never and never again shall the laws of our land rend our people apart or legalise their oppression and repression.

Inauguration speech, 10 May 1994

We must work for the day when we, as South Africans, see one another and interact with one another as equal human beings and as part of one nation united, rather than torn asunder, by its diversity.

Address to 49th session of UN, 3 October 1994

Being latecomers to freedom and democracy, we have the benefit of the experience of others.

'Renewal & Renaissance – Towards a New World Order', lecture at Oxford Centre for Islamic Studies, 11 July 1997

In the same way that the liberation of South Africa from apartheid was an achievement of Africa, the reconstruction and development of our country is part of the rebirth of the continent.

'Renewal & Renaissance – Towards a New World Order' lecture, 11 July 1997

The hard slog of reconstruction and development is as exciting as the tremors of conflict.

South Africa is a worldwide icon of the universality of human rights; of hope, peace and reconciliation.

*Heritage Day, Robben Island, 24 September
1997*

In time, we must bestow on South Africa the
greatest gift – a more humane society.

*20th anniversary of Steve Biko's death,
12 September 1997*

What we have achieved will serve as a symbol
of peace and reconciliation, and of hope, wher-
ever communities and societies are in the grip of
conflict.

*Hon Doctorate by Ben-Gurion University of the
Negev, Cape Town, 19 September 1997*

We can never be complacent, because the lega-
cies of our past still run very deeply through our
society.

*Sowetan Nation Building 10th Anniversary
speech, 30 June 1998*

We are regarded as a pioneering nation when it
comes to reaching a peaceful settlement.

South Africa has a special responsibility to work for
peace, democracy and development everywhere.

*Nelson Mandela, on the 10th anniversary of his
11 February 1990 release from prison*

Our nation comes from a history of deep division and strife; let us never through our deeds or words take our people back down that road.

Nelson Mandela was addressing the ANC and a 5 000-strong crowd at Loftus Versfeld Stadium, Pretoria, at a rally to celebrate his 90th birthday in July 2008

---

on South Africans

We are all one nation in one country.

Each one of us is as intimately attached to the soil of this beautiful country as are the famous jacaranda trees of Pretoria and the mimosa trees of the bushveld.

From his Inaugural speech, 10 May 1994

My country is rich in the minerals and gems that lie beneath its soil, but I have always known that its greatest wealth is its people, finer and truer than the purest diamonds.

It is our privilege as South Africans to be living at a time when our nation is emerging from the darkest night into the bright dawn of freedom and democracy.

Unveiling of mural celebrating the adoption of the new constitution, 8 August 1996

Pride in our country is a common bond between us all. It is the essence of our new patriotism.

Farewell for SA representatives to the Olympic Games, Atlanta, 28 June 1996

The onus is on us, through hard work, honesty and integrity, to reach for the stars.

With all our colours and races combined in one nation, we are an African people.

Address to UK parliament, 11 July 1997

Having achieved our own freedom, we can fall into the trap of washing our hands of difficulties that others face.

International Day of Solidarity with the Palestinian People, 4 December 1997

A society for centuries trampled upon by the jack-boot of inhumanity.

20th anniversary of Steve Biko's death, 12 September 1997

By joining hands South Africans have overcome problems others thought would forever haunt us.

Sowetan Nation Building 10th Anniversary speech, Johannesburg, 30 June 1998

There is no more fascinating story today than how South Africans who were enemies now work together to confound the prophets of doom who expected rivers of blood to flow across the country.

He said this shortly after returning from his valedictory tour of the US and Canada, September 1998

South Africans are conscious of their obligations to do whatever they can to contribute to the advancement of peace, democracy and justice whenever possible.

My wish is that South Africans never give up on the belief in goodness, that they cherish that faith in human beings as a cornerstone of our democracy.

Let us never be unmindful of the terrible past from which we come – that memory not as a means to keep us shackled to the past in a negative manner, but rather as a joyous reminder of how far we have come and how much we have achieved.

Nelson Mandela to a joint sitting of parliament on 10 May 2004, celebrating the 10th anniversary of democracy in South Africa

---

on sport

Sport can reach out to people in a way which politicians can't.

I have always believed that sport is a right, not a privilege.

---

on the struggle

The Struggle is my life.

From his famous press statement of 26 June 1961, whilst living underground as the Black Pimpernel

Struggle that does not strengthen organisation can lead to a blind alley.

Struggle without discipline can lead to anarchy.

Struggle without unity enables the other side to pick us off one by one.

Harlem speech 21 July 1990

No organisation whose interests are identical with those of the toiling masses will advocate conciliation to win its demands.

From Liberation, June 1953

[South Africans] displayed heroism, an incredible sense of discipline and a capacity for selflessness, as well as a quiet determination not to bend the knee to the dictates of tyrants.

The success or failure of all the campaigns against apartheid, from the 1946 African miners' strike to the resistance campaigns of the 80s, depended on a willingness to give up the comforts of life.

Running through the struggle like a golden thread is one motif – the indomitable human spirit and a moving capacity for self-sacrifice and discipline.

A willingness to make sacrifices for a loftier purpose was the unwritten code of the struggle.

No struggle can be waged effectively in isolation.

Chris Hani Award, 10th National Congress of the SACP, 1 July 1998

---

on survival

For me, survival is the ability to cope with difficulties, with circumstances, and to overcome them.

yes but what of global survival?

on talk

Rhetoric is not important. Actions are.

---

on thoughts

Thinking is one of the most important weapons in dealing with problems.

on time

Lack of punctuality is something which shows lack of respect for the organisation and those appointed into positions, and a lack of self respect.

More often than not, an epoch creates and nurtures the individuals which are associated with its twists and turns.

ANC Conference, 20 December 1997

One minute can change the world. ✔

on the Truth and Reconciliation Commission

Above all the healing process involved the nation, because it is the nation itself that needs to redeem and reconstruct itself.

The Truth and Reconciliation Commission started its work in February 1996. It heard of atrocities from the right and the left, heard testimony from murderers and torturers – and also from victims and the families of dead victims. It was intended to be an instrument of reconciliation and not revenge

All South Africans face the challenge of coming to terms with the past in ways which will enable us to face the future as a united nation at peace with itself.

Some criticise us when we say that whilst <u>we can forgive, we can never forget</u>.

Ordinary South Africans are determined that the <u>past be known, the better to ensure that it is not repeated</u>.

Incomplete and imperfect as the process may be, it shall leave us less burdened by the past and unshackled to pursue a glorious future.

This was said in his New Year's message to South Africa, 1998; it followed a harrowing year at the <u>Truth and Reconciliation Commission</u>, where the <u>country's brutal past was opened for all to see</u>. One of the last people called to give evidence before the Commission in 1997 was Winnie Madikizela-Mandela, the President's second (and former) wife

We are all bound to agonise over the price in terms of justice that the victims have to pay.

20th anniversary of Steve Biko's Death, 12 September 1997

The half-truths of a lowly interrogator cannot and should not hide the culpability of the commanders and the political leaders who gave the orders.

20th anniversary of Steve Biko's Death,
12 September 1997

on ubuntu ✓

The spirit of *ubuntu*, that profound African sense
that we are human only through the humanity
of other human beings – is not a parochial phe-
nomenon, but has added globally to our common
search for a better world.

There are numerous definitions of ubuntu –
kindness towards human beings is perhaps too
mild; as Mandela says, it is to do with one's
humanity being enriched by another's.

(Ubuntu means) that if we are to accomplish anything in this world, it will in equal measure be due
to the work and achievement of others.

Nelson Mandela wrote this in 1998 as part of
the preface to Richard Stengel's book Mandela's
Way

on unilateral decisions

We are really appalled by any country, whether
it be a superpower or a small country, that goes
outside the United Nations and attacks independent countries.

*He said this on 2 September 2002 as the USA
looked increasingly unlikely to go through the
United Nations in its pursuit of weapons of
mass destruction in Iraq. He had also tried to
phone George Bush himself (and failed), but
had phoned George Bush Snr instead: 'I asked
him to speak to his son. I have already spoken to
General Colin Powell and I am waiting to speak
to Condoleezza Rice. I have not given up trying
to persuade President Bush not to attack Iraq.'
It was also the day he awarded Nelson Mandela
scholarships to 11 post-graduate students, met
French President Jacques Chirac at his home,
telephoned US Security Adviser Condoleezza
Rice and (at 6 pm) launched the Fifth World
Parks Congress at the Nedcor building in
Sandton*

I resent any country, be it a superpower or not,
that takes a unilateral decision to attack another
country.

*Nelson Mandela was speaking on 5 September
2002, stating at the same time that there was
every reason to support the US if it attacked
Iraq, providing the action had been ratified by the
United Nations*

on the United Kingdom

I regard the British parliament as the most democratic institution in the world, and the independence and impartiality of its judiciary never fail to arouse my admiration.

From the Rivonia Treason Trial, 20 April 1964

Your right to determine your own destiny was used to deny us to determine our own.

From his speech to the House of Commons,
5 May 1993

This country has produced men and women whose names are well known in South Africa, because they, together with thousands of others of your citizens, stood up to oppose this evil system and helped to bring us to where we are today.

Speech to House of Commons, 5 May 1993

We return to this honoured place neither with pikes nor a desire for revenge nor even a plea to your distinguished selves to assuage our hunger for bread. We come to you as friends.

From his historic speech to both Houses of
Parliament, London, July 1996

In a sense, I leave a part of my being here.

*Receiving the Freedom of the City of London,
July 1996*

The UK, as one of the bastions of democracy, has an obligation to ensure that we have all the material needs to entrench democracy in our country.

I love every one of you. You must understand that the people of South Africa are very grateful to you.

*Addressing a crowd of 10 000 from the balcony
of South Africa House, Trafalgar Square,
London, July 1996*

---

on the USA

We are linked by nature, but proud of each other by choice.

*Of New York, which he visited with Winnie on
his first trip abroad after his February 1990
release, he said: 'To see it from the bottom of its
great glass-and-concrete canyons while millions
upon millions of pieces of ticker tape came
floating down was a breathtaking experience.'*

Let us keep our arms locked together so that we form a solid phalanx against racism.

Address to US Congress, 28 June 1990

The stand you took established the understanding among the millions of our people that here we have friends, here we have fighters against racism who feel hurt because we are hurt, who seek our success because they too seek the victory of democracy over tyranny.

Address to the joint Houses of Congress of the USA, September 1994

Who are they now to pretend they are the policemen of the world, the ones who should decide for the people of Iraq what should be done with their government and their leadership?

Nelson Mandela was speaking about the USA and UK's plans to invade Iraq in 1993. He accused the US of seeking Iraqi oil and accused US President George Bush and UK Prime Minister Tony Blair of undermining the UN and its Secretary-General, Kofi Annan. 'Is it because the Secretary-General of the United Nations is a black man?' he angrily asked

How can they have the arrogance to dictate to us where we should go or who our friends should be?

A heated comment made at a dinner in Johannesburg in October 1997 on the eve of his controversial visit to Libya. The USA had expressed its disapproval of the visit

on violence

Government violence can do only one thing, and that is to breed counter-violence.

'Black Man in a White Court' statement, Old Synagogue, 15 October 1962

Take your guns, your knives and your pangas, and throw them into the sea.

His first speech in the troubled province of KwaZulu-Natal after his release from prison, 25 February 1990

 People who kill children are no better than animals.

Use violence only in self-defence.

In the end, the cries of the infant who dies because of hunger or because a machete has slit open its stomach, will penetrate the noises of the modern city and its sealed windows to say: am I not human too!

From his historic speech to the Joint Houses of Parliament of the United Kingdom, 11 July 1996

We hope the world will reach a stage when it realises that the use of violence against any community is something that puts us next to animals.

Violence and non-violence are not mutually exclusive; it is the predominance of the one or the other that labels a struggle.

---

on the vote

The question of education has nothing to do with the question of the vote.

As in Zimbabwe, there was a vocal section of white voters who maintained that the vote should not be given to uneducated or barely literate people. Some form of qualification, resulting in a limited franchise, was suggested. This was rejected – as it had been in Zimbabwe – in favour of one man, one vote

A vote without food, shelter and health care would be to create the appearance of equality while actual inequality is entrenched.

Clark University Investiture, 10 July 1993

---

on white South Africans

The majority of white men regard it as the destiny of the white race to dominate the man of colour.

From the ANC Youth League Manifesto of 1944, largely written by him

White supremacy implies black inferiority.

From the dock at the Rivonia Treason Trial, 20 April 1964

Just as many whites have killed just as many blacks.

Asked about deaths of white civilians in ANC attacks, 1990

Whites fear the reality of democracy.

As long as whites think in terms of group rights they are talking the language of apartheid.

Spoken before the April 1994 elections

Whites are fellow South Africans and we want them to feel safe, and we appreciate the contribution they have made towards the development of this country.

They have had education, they have got the knowledge, skills and expertise. We want that knowledge and expertise now that we are building our country.

The whites still think as if there were no blacks, or coloureds, or Indians.

Said on his wildly successful state visit to the United Kingdom, July 1996

Our blood did not want to deal with such people ... but our brains said something else.

He was speaking in March 1999, referring
to the ANC's decision to go for a negotiated
settlement with the Nationalist government;
this led to the April 1994 general election which
brought him to his presidency

---

on women

The beauty of a woman lies as much in her face as in her body.

From a letter to his daughter Zindzi, 5 March
1978

If a pretty woman walks by, I don't want to be out of the running.

He was talking to foreign correspondent Patti
Waldmeir at the time

Women today are very sensitive to men expressing opinions without consulting them.

It's a unique woman who can turn the whole world around and make it the best living place to experience.

Nelson Mandela said this in May 2002, some
four years after his marriage to Graça Machel

For every woman and girl violently attacked, we reduce our humanity.

on work

> **Job, jobs and jobs** are the dividing line in many families between a decent life and a wretched existence.

> **Workers need a living wage** – and the right to join unions of their own choice and to participate in determining policies that affect their lives.

Soweto rally, 13 February 1990

on the world

> **The problems are such that** for anybody with a conscience who can use whatever influence he may have to try to bring about peace, it's difficult to say no.

on writing

> **Writing is a prestigious profession** which puts one right into the centre of the world and, to remain on top, one has to work really hard, the aim being a good and original theme, simplicity in expression and the use of the irreplaceable word.

From a letter to his daughter Zindzi,
4 September 1977

on xenophobia

> **Never forget the greatness** of a nation that has overcome its division. Let us never descend into destructive divisiveness.

Nelson Mandela wrote this on 13 May 2008
as South Africa struggled with xenophobic
riots countrywide. This was the headline to an
advertisement in the Sunday Times of 1 June
2008 supported by hundreds of South Africans
from Archbishop Emeritus Desmond Tutu to
Leon Geffen

on youth

I admire young people who are concerned with the affairs of their community and nation perhaps because I also became involved in struggle whist I was still at school.

Bastille Day, Paris speech, 14 July 1996

Young people are capable, when aroused, of bringing down the towers of oppression and raising the banners of freedom.

Bastille Day, 14 July Paris speech, 1996

I appeal to the youth and all those on the ground: start talking to each other across divisions of race and political organisations.

I pay tribute to the endless heroism of youth.

Address to rally in Cape Town, 11 February 1990

Whenever I am with energetic young people, I feel like a recharged battery.

Speech at the Food for Life Festival, Durban, 23 April 1997

---

on Zulus

No people can boast more proudly of having ploughed a significant field in the struggle.

Rally in Durban, 25 February 1990

Zulus have fought a long struggle against oppression.

Rally in Durban, 25 February 1990

The Battle of Isandlwana in 1879 has been an inspiration for those of us engaged in the struggle for justice and freedom in South Africa.

The battle took place under the shadow of a midday eclipse on 22 January 1879

Sources

ANC Youth League Manifesto, 1944; BBC News; *Leadership; Liberation* (June 1953); M-Net (*Funigalore*); *Saturday Star; The Star; Sunday Times; Mail & Guardian; Sowetan; The Argus; Cape Times;* SAPA; AP; *Business Day; The New York Times; Newsweek;* Reuters; *RSA Review* 1995; *The Natal Witness; Vogue* (French edition), Dec 1993/Jan 1994; *Time; The Financial Times; The Daily Telegraph; The Sunday Telegraph; The Sunday Independent; ThisDay*

The Struggle is My Life (Pathfinder, New York); *Nelson Mandela: The Man and the Movement* by Mary Benson (Penguin); *Higher than Hope* by Fatima Meer (Madiba); *The Historic Speech of Nelson Rolihlahla Mandela at the Rivonia Trial* (Learn & Teach Publications); *Rivonia – Operation Mayibuye: A Review of the Rivonia Trial* by HHW de Villiers (Afrikaanse Pers-Boekhandel); *Anatomy of a Miracle* by Patti Waldmeir (WW Norton & Company, 1997); *Madiba* (Martin Schneider), 1997; *Beyond the Miracle* by Allister Sparks (Jonathan Ball Publishers); *A Prisoner in the Garden* (Penguin/Nelson Mandela Foundation), 2005

Radio Good Hope; Radio 702; SABC; SATV (Allister Sparks' interview) 1998; Carte Blanche (M-Net)

2004; ANC Youth League Manifesto, 1944; Nelson
Mandela Foundation. 'No Easy Walk to Freedom'
speech, 21 September 1953; 'A New Menace in
Africa' speech, March 1958; Verwoerd's Tribalism
speech, May 1959; 'The Struggle is My Life' press
statement, 26 June 1961; Letter to the Prime Minister,
Dr HF Verwoerd, 26 June 1961; Address to the
Conference of the Pan-African Freedom Movement
of East and South Africa, Addis Ababa, January
1962; 'Black Man in a White Court' Trial speech,
the Old Synagogue, Pretoria, 7 November 1962;
Rivonia Treason Trial speech, 20 April 1964; Letter
to his daughter Zindzi Mandela, 4 September 1977;
Mandela's Call to the Youth of South Africa smuggled
speech, 1980; 'Whilst Still in Prison', his first speech
in almost 25 years, defiantly read by Zindzi Mandela,
10 February 1985; Release from Victor Verster Prison
speech, Cape Town, 11 February 1990; Bishopscourt
press conference, 12 February 1990; FNB Stadium
(Soccer City) speech, Johannesburg 13 February
1990; Bloemfontein speech, 25 February 1990;
Durban Rally speech, 25 February 1990; Address
to the Swedish Parliament, 13 March 1990; Harlem
speech, New York, 21 June 1990; Address to the
Joint Session of the Houses of Congress of the USA,
26 June 1990; Announcement of his separation
from Winnie, 13 April 1992; Gandhi Hall, Lenasia,
speech, 27 September 1992; Speech to the House of
Commons, United Kingdom, 5 May 1993; Acceptance
Address at the Clark University Investiture, Atlanta,
10 July 1993; Nobel Peace Prize Award Ceremony
speech, Oslo, Norway, 10 December 1993; ANC

Election Victory speech, 2 May 1994; Inauguration speech, 10 May 1994; Address to the 49th Session of the General Assembly, United Nations, 3 October 1994; Business Leaders speech, New Delhi, India, 26 January 1995; African Cup of Nations Tournament speech, 13 January 1996; Opening address to third session of Parliament, 9 February 1996; Interfaith Commissioning Service for the Truth & Reconciliation Commission speech, 13 February 1996; University of Potchefstroom speech, 19 February 1996; Opening of SA Parliament speech, 9 February 1996; Thanksgiving Service for the Ministry of Archbishop Tutu, Cape Town, 23 June 1996; SA Representatives to Olympic & Paralympic Games, Atlanta, speech, 28 June 1996; Joint Houses of Parliament Speech, London, 11 July 1996; Freedom of the City of London, Guildhall speech, 10 July 1996; Bastille Day speech, Paris, 14 July 1996; OAU Summit speech, Yaounde, 8 July 1996; 75th Anniversary of the South African Communist Party speech, 28 July 1996; Warrenton Presidential School Project speech, 30 August 1996; Signing of the SA Constitution speech, Sharpeville 10 December 1996; Food for Life, Pietermaritzburg speech, 23 April 1997; Freedom of Pietermaritzburg speech, 25 April 1997; State Banquet speech for President Museveni of Uganda, 27 May 1997; Lecture at the Oxford Centre for Islamic Studies, 11 July 1997; Commemoration of the 20th Anniversary of Steve Biko's Death speech, East London 12 September 1997; Honourary Doctorate by Ben-Gurion University of the Negev, Cape Town, 19 September 1997; Heritage Day speech, Robben Island, 24 September 1997; State

Banquet for Prime Minister Gujral of India, Cape Town 7 October 1997; Collar of the Nile Speech, Cairo, 21 October 1997; Colonel Qadhafi speech, Tripoli, 22 October 1997; Presentation of the Africa Peace Award to Mozambique, Durban, 1 November 1997; State Banquet for Prince Charles speech, Cape Town, 4 November 1997; Foreign Correspondents Association speech, Johannesburg, 21 November 1997; Freedom of the City of Cape Town speech, 27 November 1997; Regina Mundi Day speech, Soweto, 30 November 1997; Bram Fischer Memorial Trust speech, Bloemfontein, 28 November 1997; International Day of Solidarity with the Palestinian People speech, Pretoria, 4 December 1997; Farewell as President of the ANC speech, Mafikeng, 20 December 1997; OAU Heads of State & Government speech, Ouagadougou, Burkina Faso, 8 June 1998; Freedom of the City of Cardiff, speech, Cardiff, Wales, 16 June 1998; Sowetan Nation Building 10th Anniversary speech, Johannesburg, 30 June 1998; Chris Hani Award speech, 10th National Congress of the South African Communist Party, Johannesburg, 1 July 1998; Closing ceremony speech at the 19th Meeting of Heads of Government of the Caribbean Community, St Lucia, 4 July 1998; State banquet for President Rawlings of Ghana speech, Pretoria, 9 July 1998; Aids Speech, Paris, 14 July 2003; International Year of Older Persons speech, Cape Town, 17 July 2003; '46664 Give One Minute of Your Life to Aids' speech, 21 October 2003